SIR TONY ROBINSON'S
WORLD WAR I AND WORLD WAR II

Sir Tony Robinson has been scribbling away since he was old enough to pick up a pencil. He's written long stuff (like a history of Australia), and shorter stuff (like this). He's rewritten old stories (like the ones about the Greek heroes Odysseus and Theseus), and made up new ones (for instance his children's TV series *Tales from Fat Tulip's Garden*). But history is what he likes best, because he says, 'How do you know who you are if you don't know where you came from?' That's why he's written Sir Tony Robinson's Weird World of Wonders, and he doesn't want to stop until he's written about every single bit of history there's ever been - although in order to do this he'll have to live till he's 8,374!

Del Thorpe has been drawing ever since that time he ruined his mum's best tablecloth with wax crayons. Most of his formative work can be found in the margins of his old school exercise books. His maths teacher described these misunderstood works as 'wasting time'. When he left normal school, Del wen[t] ... grown-up t... was m... ...oons a...

D1342804

Books by Sir Tony Robinson

Sir Tony Robinson's Weird World of Wonders series

British

Egyptians

Greeks

Pets

Romans

World War I

World War II

Bad Kids

The Worst Children's Jobs in History

SIR TONY ROBINSON'S

WEIRD WORLD OF WONDERS

WORLD WAR I AND WORLD WAR II

2 BOOKS IN 1

Illustrated
by
Del Thorpe

MACMILLAN CHILDREN'S BOOKS

First published 2013 in two separate volumes as *Sir Tony Robinson's Weird World of Wonders: World War I*
and *Sir Tony Robinson's Weird World of Wonders: World War II* by Macmillan Children's Books

This edition published 2015 by Macmillan Children's Books
an imprint of Pan Macmillan
a division of Macmillan Publishers Limited
20 New Wharf Road, London N1 9RR
Associated companies throughout the world
www.panmacmillan.com

ISBN 978-1-4472-8492-5

Text copyright © Sir Tony Robinson 2013
Illustrations copyright © Del Thorpe 2013

1 3 5 7 9 8 6 4 2

A CIP catalogue record for this book is available from the British Library.

Typeset by Dan Newman/Perfect Bound Ltd
Printed and bound by CPI Group (UK) Ltd, Croydon CRO 4YY

Thanks to . . .

If you turn to page 314 you'll find the name **Gaby Morgan** in tiny writing (in fact everyone who helped me with this book is in tiny writing except me, because I RULE THE WORLD!). Gaby is my editor, which means she tells me which bits of my books are rubbish and then makes me rewrite them. She's the biggest ever supporter of Weird World of Wonders, and is the best editor I could possibly have (although don't tell her I said that, please). Working with her is quite tough, but very interesting and lots of fun. Maybe I'll put her name in slightly bigger writing next time. Or maybe not.

I'm quite good at storytelling and making up jokes, but my researcher **Jessica Cobb** is a human search engine. If I ask her a question, her brain starts to whirr, steam comes out of her ears and she flips open her laptop, gets on the phone or rushes out of the room and sprints down to the library. Half an hour later she's back again, handing me the most brilliant, detailed answer ever. If I run out of cash I'll sell her to Google. They'll probably pay about a million pounds for her, and it'll be good value for money. Thank you, Jess.

Picture Credits

t = top; b = bottom; l = left; r = right

Pages 5, 47, 97, 100 Getty/Roger Viollet; 9, 39, 92, 106 Getty/Time & Life Pictures; 12 Shutterstock/Crepesoles; 13 Getty/De Agostini; 14, 83, 123, 126, 140 Getty Images; 16, 23, 26, 35, 51, 61, 64, 75, 86, 98, 101, 104, 107, 109, 112, 114, 115, 117, 119, 120, 127, 132, 143, 144 Getty/Hulton Archive; 17, 45, 80, 88, 95, 99, 121, 125, 129, 138, 142 (x2), 145 Getty/Popperfoto; 18 Shutterstock/tab62; 20 Shutterstock/Sourabh; 21, 30, 58, 65, 84 Getty/UIG; 24 Getty/British Library/Robana; 29 Official British Military photograph. First published in *The Great War*, ed. H. W. Wilson, 1916; 34 Getty/Fairfax Media; 44 Shutterstock/3drenderings; 54 Shutterstock/gresei, Shutterstock/Brenda Carson; 55 Shutterstock/spirit of america; 60, 150 Shutterstock/Eric Isselee; 62, 128 Getty/Gamma-Keystone; 70 Shutterstock/Gary Blakeley; 81 Shutterstock/Jeroen van den Broek (dog), Shutterstock/Viorel Sima (man); 85 Shutterstock/Basphoto; 87 Shutterstock/Fedorov Oleksiy; 90 Shutterstock/YurkaImmortal; 94, 146 Getty/IWM; 102 Shutterstock/WDG Photo; 105 US Library of Congress; 118 Shutterstock/Hang Dinh (tl), Shutterstock/mikhail (tr), Shutterstock/Sadik Gulec (bl & br); 121 Shutterstock/Jubal Harshaw; 124 Shutterstock/Iakov Filimonov, Shutterstock/Accent; 125 Shutterstock/Lienhard.illustrator; 134 Shutterstock/Margo Harrison; 148 With the very kind permission of the granddaughters of Pte George Ellison; 149 Tony Robinson; 150 Shutterstock/vector work.

Hello, we're the Curiosity Crew. You'll probably spot us hanging about in this book checking stuff out.

It's about blood, guts, mud, moustaches and millions of men making a military mess across half the world.

Read on to find out more . . .

Grace

Peewee   Stig   Jojo

Nits

INTRODUCTION

Ever since the olden days . . .

. . . the handsome prince raised his mighty sword . . .

Oooh!

. . . people have loved hearing stories about war.

. . . 'CHARGE' roared the evil emperor . . .

Aaaah!

Admittedly most of them had
never actually been to war ...

... but the
bravest of the
knights stood his
ground ...

Eeeeeh!

... and didn't have a clue
what it was really like.

... he sliced through
the emperor's armour,
sending his severed head
flying through the air!

But it all sounded exciting, heroic and full of glory!

Ahem!

But in 1914 World War One began, and that changed everything.

Suddenly hundreds of thousands of young men had to go to war, and they didn't like what they found when they got there. No excitement, no heroics and definitely no glory; instead . . .

And just to make things even more gruesome, a load of horrible machines and chemicals specially designed to kill people.

So, mixed up in all the mud were lots of bits of dead bodies and gallons of blood.

It was horrific. Some people called it the 'Great War'; others said it was . . .

But how did it start? How many people died? And who won?

If you'd like to know, turn the page . . .

CHAPTER ONE

HOW IT ALL STARTED

To the Black Hand Gang.
Read and Destroy.

Mission — assassinate the heir
to the Austro-Hungarian throne.

Date — 28th June 1914

Place — Sarajevo, Bosnia,
Eastern Europe.

Archduke Franz Ferdinand was a seriously important man. When his uncle died he'd become emperor of the massively powerful Austro-Hungarian Empire, which meant he'd rule over millions of people. So when he arrived in Sarajevo (pronounced 'Sa-ra-yey-vo') on a state visit, crowds lined the streets to catch a glimpse of him in his flashy uniform and his big hat with green feathers on it.

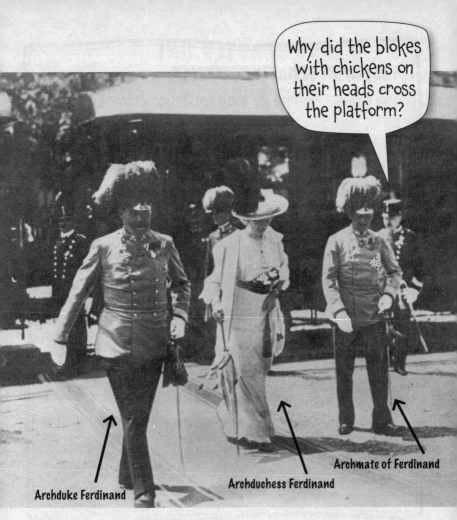

Archduke Ferdinand

Archduchess Ferdinand

Archmate of Ferdinand

Little did they know that among the crowd were six armed killers on a deadly mission. They were members of the 'Black Hand' – a band of young Serbian men who loathed the Austro-Hungarian Empire and were determined that their little country of Serbia wasn't going to become part of it.

THE EMPIRE OF NASTY SQUABBLES

Take a look at this map and you'll see that huge chunks of
Europe were once part of the mighty 'Austro-Hungarian' Empire.
More than 50 million people lived in it, speaking fifteen different
languages. It was big and powerful, but it caused lots of
squabbles, some of which got very nasty indeed.

Germany

Poland

Russia

Austria-Hungary

Romania

Switzerland

Italy

Serbia

Don't invade
us, we're only
little!

Their mission was to kill Franz Ferdinand, and because
no one in Sarajevo was expecting trouble, there were
hardly any police or soldiers about. It looked as though
this job was going to be as easy as squashing a fly.

But it
wasn't!

The first gang-member was just about to throw his grenade at the Archduke's car when a policeman wandered over to him. So the would-be assassin pretended he was an innocent bystander and walked away.

Franz Ferdinand's car passed the second gang-member, but he couldn't get his grenade out of his pocket in time, and the royal party drove on.

The third one managed to throw his grenade, but it bounced off the roof of the Archduke's vehicle and blew up the car behind.

Two more of these incompetent killers lost their nerve and ran away.

The last member of the gang, nineteen-year-old Gavrilo Princip, was really upset that their mission had failed, so he went off to a nearby cafe for a nice cup of coffee. But just as he was biting into his cinnamon and apple pastry . . .

We don't actually know that Gavrilo had a cinnamon and apple pastry, but it makes the whole scene a bit more dramatic, doesn't it?

No!

. . . the Archduke's car pulled up right beside him. Gavrilo jumped out of his seat, fired his gun at the Archduke and his wife . . . and shot them dead!

Even this murder attempt nearly failed because Franz Ferdinand was wearing a bullet-proof vest. But he was shot in the neck, so it didn't protect him!

The Archduke's assassination, drawn by someone who wasn't there

Whoops!

Not me!

Even though Franz Ferdinand's murder was horrific, who would have thought it would lead to the death of millions of people?

13

WHAT HAPPENED NEXT...?

The leaders of the Austro-Hungarian Empire were furious that some pipsqueak Serbian had bumped off the heir to their throne, so they declared war on Serbia. But it didn't stop there.

Austria-Hungary was friends with the Germans, so Germany joined in.

Germany was friends with the Turks, so Turkey joined in.

14

Serbia was friends with the Russians, so Russia joined in.

Russia was friends with the French, so France joined in.

And France was friends with the British, so Britain joined in.

Pretty soon the assassination at Sarajevo had turned into one almighty punch-up involving all the major superpowers of the time!

On one side were the 'Central Powers', including Austria-Hungary, Germany and Turkey.

Austrian troops march through Vienna in 1914

We'll beat those Brits in a week.

You sure?

The 1st Battalion of the Mid-Kent
Volunteers march through Tunbridge Wells
in 1914

On the other were the
'Allies', including
Britain, Russia and France.

THE BEST OF FRIENDS . . . ?

The war was a huge surprise. Nobody could believe that so many European countries were fighting each other, particularly as most of the kings and queens were part of the same big family. This was all down to Queen Victoria of Britain, her nine children and her forty grandchildren who, like posh people everywhere, wanted to marry people as posh as they were – which meant other kings, queens, princes and princesses.

Happy Christmas Mummy from **Victoria** and **Frederick III, Emperor of Germany**

Happy Christmas Mummy from **Alice** and **Louis IV, Grand Duke of Hesse**

Happy Christmas Mummy from **Albert Edward (King Edward VIII of Britain)** and **Princess Alexandra of Denmark**

Happy Christmas Mummy from **Alfred** and **Grand Duchess Maria Alexandrovna of Russia**

Happy Christmas Granny from **Emperor Wilhelm III of Germany**

Happy Christmas Granny from **King George V of Britain**

Happy Christmas Granny from **Alexandra, Empress of Russia**

Happy Christmas Granny from **Marie, Queen of Romania**

Happy Christmas Granny

Happy Christmas Granny from **Maud, Queen of Norway**

Happy Christmas Granny

Happy Christmas Granny

Happy Christmas Granny

Happy Christmas Granny

Happy Christmas Granny

Happy Christmas Granny

About half the crowned heads of Europe were cousins, second cousins and third cousins once removed. They held family parties, sent each other Christmas cards and appeared to be the best of friends.

Happy Christmas Mummy from **Helena** and **Prince Christian of Schleswig-Holstein**

Happy Christmas Mummy from **Arthur** and **Princess Louise Margaret of Prussia**

Happy Christmas Mummy from **Leopold** and **Princess Helena of Waldeck & Pyrmont**

Happy Christmas Mummy from **Beatrice** and **Prince Henry of Battenberg**

Happy Christmas Mummy from **Louise** and **John Campbell, Marquess of Lorne**

Happy Christmas Granny from **Margaret, Crown Princess of Sweden**

Happy Christmas Granny

Happy Christmas Granny from **Victoria, Queen of Spain**

Happy Christmas Granny

Happy Christmas Granny

Happy Christmas Granny

Happy Christmas Granny

Happy Christmas Granny

Happy Christmas Granny

Happy Christmas Granny

Happy Christmas Granny

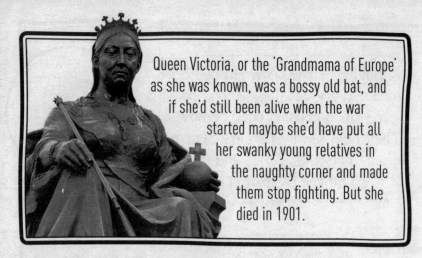

Queen Victoria, or the 'Grandmama of Europe' as she was known, was a bossy old bat, and if she'd still been alive when the war started maybe she'd have put all her swanky young relatives in the naughty corner and made them stop fighting. But she died in 1901.

WOO HOO – A WAR!

In August 1914, on the day war was declared, people across Europe poured into the streets to celebrate. Londoners gathered in front of Buckingham Palace to cheer, wave flags and sing the National Anthem. It might sound totally bonkers to you and me, but to many people at the time the war seemed a jolly good idea.

Just like today, most people lived ordinary lives in ordinary towns where nothing much happened that was remotely interesting. But now a big war was about to start just like they'd heard about in adventure stories. It was a chance for young men to be heroes, win glory and see the world. Best of all they'd get to teach those jumped-up Johnny Foreigners a lesson they'd never forget – hurrah!

King George V and the Royal Family watch a battalion leaving for France, August 1914

Of course, nobody considered for a moment that they might die . . .

. . . or that the Johnny Foreigners might turn out to be rather good at fighting!

They also didn't expect the war to last long – most people thought they'd be back home in time to put up the Christmas decorations. But they were seriously wrong!

. . . THE WORST OF ENEMIES!

Wilhelm II was the Emperor (or Kaiser) of Germany. He was one of Queen Victoria's many grandchildren, but he wasn't a nice grandchild: he hated the fact that Britain was powerful and had its own Empire. He was also vain, aggressive, tactless, boastful and rude, and called his granny the 'old hag'! Not surprisingly, Victoria couldn't stand him.

He encouraged Germany to build a big navy to challenge the British at sea. Britain and Germany had once been friends, but now they were the worst of enemies.

Kaiser Wilhelm II in the uniform of the 'Deathshead Hussars'

The chief officer in the British Army was Field Marshal Horatio Herbert Kitchener. He was a mighty hero with a big bushy moustache, who'd led his troops at the Battle of Omdurman in Africa where they'd won a famous victory!

Actually it was a famous victory which involved loads of British soldiers equipped with machine guns wiping out more than 9,000 Sudanese warriors armed with nothing but spears.

That's not very heroic, is it!

Kitchener had a niggling feeling that this war might be a bit different...

...because this time the enemy would be equipped with more than just spears!

... and he wasn't convinced the war would be over by Christmas. In fact he suspected it would last for years and that lots of people would get killed. He reckoned that Britain would only be able to win if it had a really big army.

He needed lots of young men to join up quickly, so masses of posters were printed with his big serious face staring out of them, and the words 'Your Country Needs You' in big letters – if that didn't scare people into volunteering, he didn't know what would.

But Britain's men didn't need scaring. They were simply itching to sign up. Kitchener had thought he'd be able to recruit 100,000 soldiers, but within two months a massive 750,000 had volunteered!

By the end of World War One over 5 million British men had joined the army!

I'm actually only 16.

Nice disguise, mate!

My name's really Maud.

You naughty girl!

BOY SOLDIERS

It wasn't just men who joined up; plenty of boys did as well, some as young as twelve! To fight abroad, soldiers were supposed to be over nineteen, but lots of boys lied about their age, and in all the excitement recruiting officers often didn't bother to check their birth certificates before signing them up.

Some eager lads wore their Sunday suits or their dad's clothes to make them look older. Others gave fake names so that their parents wouldn't be able to find them and drag them back home.

COMPULSORY MOUSTACHES

Boy soldiers and women were pretty easy to spot – they were the ones without moustaches.

(Guess which one's the man)

It was a rule that all members of the British Army had to grow one, because moustaches looked so manly.

They look dogly too!

Women weren't allowed to be soldiers, but that didn't stop nineteen-year-old Dorothy Lawrence. When she was told she couldn't go to the front as a war reporter, she got hold of an army uniform, put a pair of socks down her trousers, cut her hair and cycled to the front line with forged identity papers which said she was Private Denis Smith! Unfortunately ten days later she was discovered and sent back home.

Anyone found shaving their upper lip was severely punished.

Eventually in 1916 this rule was dropped on the order of Lieutenant-General Sir Nevil Macready. This was partly because growing a moustache was a stupid thing to make people do, but also because Sir Nevil hated his own moustache so much.

It's like the small brushes with which kitchen maids and others clean saucepans.

He actually said that!

YOU'RE IN THE ARMY NOW

Soldiers were arranged into battalions of about 1,000 men.

That's wrong! Battalions started off with about 1,000 men, but after they'd been in a few battles, most had a lot less!

Brothers, cousins, friends, neighbours and workmates from the same town or village signed up together and formed what became known as 'Pals' battalions, because all the men in them knew each other. Ex-pupils from the same school formed battalions. So did professional footballers; even football supporters like the West Ham Pals!

Just imagine the whole Man U team and their fans forming a battalion and going off to Afghanistan!

KIT

Soldiers on both sides were issued with masses of kit, including:

Uniform – a grey-brown 'khaki' colour which blended into muddy landscapes. For a while British soldiers were the only ones to wear khaki. For the first few months of the war the French wore fancy blue coats and bright red trousers, until they realized this made them stick out like clowns at a funeral.

Webbing – a 'web' of straps that fastened round your chest and contained pockets and a rucksack to carry all your gear, including a water bottle, ammunition pouches, food, weapons and a blanket. Full up, your rucksack weighed as much as a ten-year-old boy! Imagine carrying one of those on your back all day!

Puttees (which means bandages) – these were strips of wool cloth that you wrapped round the bottom of your trousers to keep the mud and water from getting into the tops of your boots.

Steel Helmet – until 1915 soldiers wore a cloth or leather cap, but it quickly became obvious that you needed something more to protect your head from all those sharp bits of hot flying metal!

Scarf – hand-knitted by wives and mothers back home and sent out to the troops to help keep them warm, along with socks, mittens, balaclavas, woolly hats and sweaters!

Greatcoat – big, heavy and made of wool to keep you warm at night, with a collar or a cape to protect you from the rain. Got even heavier once you'd been standing out in the wet for a while, and took days to dry out.

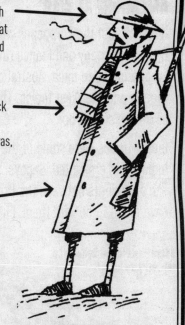

Bayonet – fixed on to the end of a rifle so you could stab somebody if they got too close. Also used for digging holes, toasting bread, opening cans, poking fires and scraping mud off your uniform.

Rifle – this was a soldier's main weapon. Its long barrel helped make it more accurate. You could shoot someone over 1,000 metres away!

Tinned Food – invented in the nineteenth century as a way of keeping food fresh. Meals included corned beef, Irish stew, and pork and beans. The French army had tinned chicken in wine, and the Italians were given tinned spaghetti Bolognese!

Entrenching Tool – perhaps the most important piece of kit. A shovel that soldiers used to dig graves, holes for toilets and most importantly miles and miles of trenches . . .

AN EMPIRE AT WAR

It wasn't just the Europeans who went to war. Many countries like Britain, Germany and France ruled over huge empires. The British Empire included India, Australia, New Zealand, Kenya, South Africa, Nigeria and the West Indies. Thousands of men from all these countries signed up.

Indian troops were some of the first to be sent to fight – 161,000 Indian soldiers called 'Sepoys' arrived in Europe in September 1914. The arguments between the British and the Germans didn't really have much to do with them, but lots of them fought heroically.

Australians leave Sydney on their way to Egypt

Crikey, there's hardly room to light the barbie!

Who farted?

Gurkhas about to leave for France

Say cheese!

You must be joking.

During the Indian Corps' first battle, a Sepoy called Usman Khan was awarded a medal after he was wounded twice, continued to fire on the enemy and absolutely refused to leave his post. Then he was wounded again, and had both his legs almost blown off, but he still wouldn't leave the battlefield till he was dragged away protesting!

Although they risked their legs and their lives for the Empire, most colonial troops faced racism. Soldiers from the West Indies and Africa were called names, given poor equipment and had to do all the worst jobs like digging trenches, carrying supplies and cleaning the army bogs.

No wonder lots of them wished they'd stayed home and let the stupid Europeans fight it out among themselves.

CHAPTER TWO

DEADMAN'S DITCH!

At the beginning of the war Germany was almost completely surrounded by its enemies, Russia, France and Britain. But the Germans had a plan, and it was very simple.

They'd beat up their next-door neighbour France ...

... turn round and attack Russia ...

... and the British would be so frightened, they'd give in and beg for mercy.

So to put the first part of their plan into action, they invaded France. The British and French Armies tried to stop them, but within a month the German Army had practically reached Paris. The French military governor needed more troops to defend the front line, but there were no military vehicles available.

So he had a brainwave. He ordered a cab . . . well, more than one, actually.

Taxi drivers from all over Paris met at the city centre, and soldiers piled into them. Within two days, Parisian cabbies had dropped off 6,000 men at the battlefield, enough to stop the enemy in its tracks!

The German advance had been halted, but the Germans didn't retreat. Instead they dug long lines of trenches to protect themselves from a counter-attack. The British and French didn't know what to do, but while they were trying to work it out, they dug trenches too.

It was the start of **three years** of horrendous, bloody trench warfare.

HOW TO BUILD A TRENCH

1) Wait for nightfall – you don't want to work in daylight in full view of the enemy . . . that would be suicide!

2) Roll up your sleeves and start digging – there are no digging machines or dumper trucks: just you, your mates and some shovels. Stand in a line and shovel out the earth until you've dug a straight-sided trench ten feet deep and six feet wide . . . Phew!

3) Get in the trench – the sooner you're in, the safer you'll be. Now take turns to dig out the ends to make the trench longer.

4) Keep changing direction – you want your trench to be a zigzag shape, not one long line. That way, if the enemy manages to get in it, they won't be able to shoot all the way down it and kill everybody at once. And if a bomb hits, the explosion won't blow everyone up!

We also do decking for patios.

Germans in a very well-made trench

5) Fix planks of wood to the sides – this stops the trench collapsing and burying you alive. For extra protection put sandbags along the top to catch any stray bullets.

6) Put up rolls of barbed wire in front of it – this will slow the attackers down when they charge towards you.

And to slow them down even more, make sure you've got a few machine guns handy.

7) Dig another trench behind it – so if the front trench is captured by the enemy, there'll be another one handy for you to jump into.

The soldiers didn't just dig one trench, they dug hundreds. Soon the two sides had built a network of over 25,000 miles of them stretching from the English Channel all the way to Switzerland. There were so many that, in order to make sure the soldiers didn't get lost, signposts were put up, and the trenches were given names like 'Rats' Alley', 'Casualty Corner' and 'Deadman's Ditch'!

GROSS-OUT IN THE TRENCHES

The Germans were planning to stay put, so their trenches were built to last, with concrete bunkers, furniture, running water, electric lights, wallpaper, carpets and even doorbells!

But the British Generals wanted to attack the Germans right away, and they were worried that if their trenches were too cosy, their men might not want to leave them. So they made sure that the British trenches were not only basic, but . . .

GROSS! **GROSS!** *GROSS!*

They were gross because they were cold, dirty and wet. In winter the temperature dropped below freezing. Soldiers got frostbite and lost their fingers and toes.

Double gross because when it rained, the trenches flooded. Their boots got soaked and their feet started to rot. If they couldn't get them dry again, their legs would get so rotten the doctors would have to cut them off!

Treble gross because the trenches stank of decaying bodies, poo, rotting food and stagnant water.

Quadruple gross because of the rats. Swarms of them fed off the rubbish and the dead bodies. One soldier woke up in the middle of the night to see two rats on his bed fighting over a severed hand!

Some rats were the size of cats and would try to eat a wounded man if he was too weak to defend himself!

There was no running water, so they couldn't have a nice hot shower and get clean . . .

Soldiers spent weeks in the same clothes . . .

Lice lived on their skin and laid eggs in the seams of their uniforms . . .

And they were likely to catch horrible diseases like cholera and typhus.

Yuck!

43

BRASS KNUCKLES

The ground between the two sets of trenches was known as 'no-man's-land'. It was covered with barbed wire, landmines, craters and dead bodies. To attack the enemy you had to cross it and risk being shot to pieces.

Sometimes hundreds of soldiers charged over it to try to force the enemy back. At other times, small groups conducted night raids to seize or destroy enemy equipment and collect information about how many people were in the trench opposite and how many guns they had. On night raids soldiers blackened their faces with burnt cork, and carried weapons that didn't make any noise, like clubs, knives, hatchets and brass knuckles.

Brass knuckles were lumps of metal that fitted over your fingers so you could give your enemy a killer punch.

Canadians in some French mud, 1917

THE DEVIL'S ROPE

In 1860 an American farmer called Joseph F. Glidden was looking for a cheap and easy way to fence off his land to stop cows from trampling through it. He came up with the idea of surrounding it with strings of twisted wire covered in sharp wire points. These fences were so vicious that the Native Americans called them the 'Devil's rope'.

In World War One, rows and rows of the horrible stuff were strung out in front of the trenches. It was difficult to blow a hole in them, and the only way to cut through them was with a pair of wire cutters.

Teams of men called 'wiring parties' were sent out at night to cut paths through the enemy's fences. They had to do it in total silence and in the pitch dark while handling sharp tools. You didn't live long if you were a member of a wiring party!

DON'T FALL ASLEEP!
DON'T GET LOST!

Discipline was strict. If you got drunk and were caught, you were tied to a wheel or a stake for several hours, sometimes in range of the enemy guns! The punishment for falling asleep on sentry duty, or for being a coward, or disobeying an order, was death by firing squad!

In September 1914, a nineteen-year-old called Thomas Highgate was found hiding in a barn. He said he'd got lost during a battle and was trying to find his way back to rejoin his unit. But he couldn't prove it because there were no witnesses; all his comrades had been killed or captured. So he was executed, and became the first British soldier to be shot for desertion.

FOOTBALL IN NO-MAN'S-LAND

It was pretty tiresome if someone fired a pot-shot at you every time you took a peek over the top of your trench. So sometimes soldiers on opposing sides would agree to have little truces. For instance they might decide not to fire at one another during breakfast, or not to throw grenades at each other's toilets.

Being shot at when you're like this is particularly annoying.

Sometimes after very heavy rain, the two sides would arrange a truce so they could pump the water out of their trenches. They did the same thing after a battle so they could collect their dead from no-man's-land.

On Christmas Day 1914, a big truce took place along large parts of the front line. German soldiers put up little Christmas trees along their trenches, and both sides sang carols and shouted 'Merry Christmas' to each other. Some soldiers got out of their trenches and exchanged cigarettes and presents! A few even got together and played a game of football in no-man's-land, with helmets for goalposts.

The Germans won 3-2!

The Generals weren't too pleased when they heard about this. Fighting started again the next day, and the following year sentries on both sides were told to shoot anyone who tried to have another truce!

WORLD WAR ONE SLANG

Ordinary British soldiers had their own special language. Here are some key words . . .

Blighty – Britain. From the Hindu word 'Vilayati', meaning a foreign country. Originally used by British troops in India. Later a 'Blighty' meant a wound so bad that it would get you sent home.

Boche – A German soldier. From the French 'caboche', meaning 'blockhead'!

Brass Hat – A high-ranking officer. Officers often wore brass-coloured braid on their hats.

Bully Beef – Canned corned beef found in ration packs. From the French 'bouillie' meaning 'boiled'.

Hun – Another word for a German soldier. The original Huns were a tribe from Asia who attacked Europe in the fifth century. In a speech in 1900 Kaiser Wilhelm compared the German Army to the Huns and it quickly became their nickname.

Kraut – Yet another word for a German soldier. Short for 'sauerkraut' which means 'pickled cabbage' (a dish which for some reason the Germans found very tasty).

Napoo – Dead, as in *'If we don't get out of here fast we'll all be napoo.'* From the French phrase *'Il n'y en à plus'* meaning *'There isn't any more'*, which the British thought sounded like *'napoo'*.

Old Sweat – An experienced soldier.

Tommy – A British soldier. Came from the name 'Tommy Atkins', which was used as an example name on British Army forms, a bit like 'Joe Bloggs' today.

Trench Rabbit – A rat.

HIDEOUS MONSTERS

After a while the Allied soldiers began to realize that the enemy were just ordinary, decent blokes like themselves, but back home their families didn't. They thought the Germans were baby-murdering monsters.

The Germans cut the hands off tiny Belgian children!

No they didn't! That's a load of rubbish!

Exactly. But when countries are at war, their governments want the army to think the enemy are bloodthirsty maniacs. Their soldiers might not want to do any more killing if they know the other side are just ordinary people.

Yeah, that's why they spread horrible rumours about them. It's called 'propaganda', and it can be really effective.

Yeah! Dead effective!

The Germans bayonet babies!

In Britain, the government encouraged newspapers to write gruesome stories about the Germans, and printed posters showing them as scary devils.

It didn't matter if the stories weren't true, as long as they made people hate the enemy.

Anything German was suddenly HORRIBLY HORRENDOUSLY BAD.

In Britain, German people were beaten up. In Australia, towns and streets with German-sounding names were renamed.

DACHSHUND

German dogs like me had stones thrown at them!

GERMAN SHEPHERD DOG

I had to change my name to Alsatian!

And in America, hamburgers...

... were renamed 'liberty sandwiches'.

Frankfurters...

... became 'liberty sausages'.

And German measles became 'liberty measles'!

Even the British King and Queen changed their name to make themselves sound less German! Their surname had been 'Saxe-Coburg' but they altered it to 'Windsor', and they're still called Windsor to this day!

Call me Elizabeth Saxe-Coburg and I'll deck you

BLOWN TO PIECES

For the best part of four years the Germans were stuck in their trenches, peering out at the British and their allies . . .

1914

. . . while the British were stuck in their trenches peering back at the Germans and their allies.

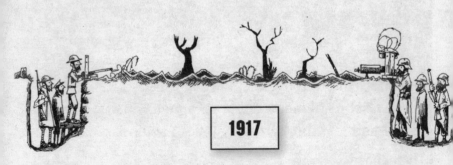

1917

Occasionally there was a big battle, but no one was really winning – at this rate the war would still be going on a hundred years later. How could the stalemate be broken? The Generals on both sides decided they needed bigger, better and nastier weapons.

WEAPONS OF MASS DESTRUCTION

Massive guns were developed which fired enormous shells.

They were full of explosives, blasted massive holes in the ground and were designed to destroy the enemy defences. And to make them even nastier some were filled with bits of metal called 'shrapnel', which would fly out and tear through human flesh and bone.

The explosions from these guns were so loud they could make your ears bleed and, even if you weren't hit by a shell or bits of flying metal, the shockwaves from the blast itself could stop your heart and rupture your insides, leaving you dead without a mark on you!

The most famous German super-gun was called . . . **BIG BERTHA**!

Big Bertha weighed as much as four double-decker buses!

Her shells were the size of dustbins, they weighed over 900 kg and she could fire them nine miles, high enough and far enough to go right over Mount Everest!

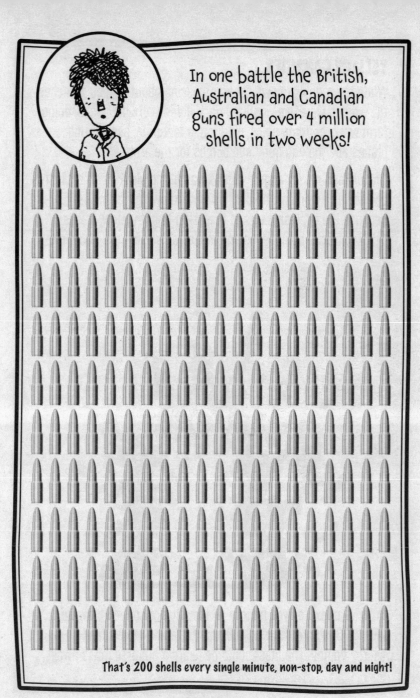

In one battle the British, Australian and Canadian guns fired over 4 million shells in two weeks!

That's 200 shells every single minute, non-stop, day and night!

YELLOW CANARIES

While the men were away at war messing about in their trenches, the women were working hard back home – driving buses, doing farm work, building ships, working in factories, assembling planes and making guns and bombs for the army.

One of their most dangerous jobs was filling shells with explosive powder. The women who did this were known as 'canaries', because the explosive turned their skin bright yellow. It was extremely poisonous and made you so sick you could die.

The explosives also had a tendency to go . . .

In 1917 an explosives factory on the edge of London blew up, killing 73 people, injuring 400 and flattening more than 900 nearby homes. The blast could be heard a hundred miles away!

An Indian Maxim team defending Egypt from the Turkish Army

DODGING BULLETS

An even more terrifying weapon was the machine gun, invented by Hiram Maxim in the 1880s.

At that time, even the most efficient guns could only fire half a dozen bullets, after which they had to be reloaded by hand. But Maxim's gun automatically fired hundreds of bullets one after the other. Even if you were a complete idiot you could become a bloodthirsty killer with no training whatsoever; all you had to do was keep your finger on the trigger!

The British Army bought lots of Maxim's guns, so the Austrians, Germans, Italians, Swiss and Russians bought lots too, and Maxim became a millionaire! By the time World War One broke out, all the major armies had machine guns. They were incredibly effective on the battlefield, killing tens of thousands of soldiers.

THE BATTLE THAT WENT HORRIBLY WRONG

In 1916 the British army planned a big attack on the German trenches near the River Somme in France. A week before it began, the Brits began firing their super-guns at the German trenches.

They had 1,500 of these massive weapons, and let loose 1.5 million shells. They were absolutely confident this bombardment would smash the enemy to pieces. They thought that when the guns stopped, they'd be able to wander over to the enemy positions, and the few quaking, terrified Germans who were still alive would throw down their weapons and run away.

But from the moment the first Brits popped their heads over the top of their trenches and started to walk across no-man's-land it became obvious that the plan had gone horribly wrong.

They hadn't destroyed the German trenches, which were very deep and well protected, and most of the enemy soldiers were alive and kicking. To make matters worse, the week-long bombardment had given the Germans plenty of warning that they were going to be attacked. When the British approached, the German machine-gunners opened fire and almost 20,000 British soldiers were killed! Another 38,000 were missing or wounded.

THE FIRE-BREATHING MONSTER

The very first flamethrower was invented over 2,000 years ago. Air was pumped into one end of a huge metal syringe, which spewed out tongues of flame from the other end.

But in 1901 the Germans came up with a modern version. It sprayed a continuous stream of oil out of the end of a tube, which, when lit by a spark, turned the oil into a terrifying stream of flame which could travel up to eighteen metres!

In World War One these fire-breathing monsters were used in the trenches. Anyone who had any sense legged it before they were burned alive.

GAS

Poison gas sounds really scary, doesn't it? But the gases used at the start of World War One were a bit pathetic. They made your enemy's eyes water and caused them to sneeze a lot, but that was about it. In other words they were rather annoying but certainly not deadly.

British gas victims in 1918

But then in 1915 the Germans started using chlorine gas. Chlorine is the stuff in your mum and dad's liquid bleach which they use to clean the toilet. It's great for killing tiny bugs that spread disease, but as any sensible kid knows, you don't want to play with it.

Chlorine gas is just as dangerous. It burns your throat and lungs, and causes you to suffocate to death very slowly. It was first released at a place called Ypres (pronounced 'Eep-rah'). Yellow-green clouds of the stuff drifted across the battlefield towards the French who, at first, thought it was just smoke. Then they started to cough and splutter and clutch their throats. Green froth spewed from their mouths and they keeled over in agony. Many died within minutes.

Chlorine gas was deadly, but if you released it when the wind was blowing in the wrong direction, you'd end up running away from your own gas.

I'm always running away from my own gas!

WEEING ON SOCKS

At first soldiers didn't have gas masks to protect them. Instead they were told that if a cloud of chlorine gas came towards them they should take off one of their socks, pee on it and put it over their mouths!

I do that too sometimes!

This is rubbish!

That may sound disgusting and a bit weird, but wee contains a chemical called ammonia, which was supposed to stop the chlorine damaging your lungs.

Soon, though, scientists came up with less sick-making methods of protection. Early gas masks were simply cloth bags with eyeholes that you put over your head. The bag was soaked in a special chemical, which helped neutralize the poison gas.

A bit better, I suppose.

Wicked, man!

But then they invented a 'box respirator', a gas mask connected to a box with a hose in the middle. The box filtered the air and made it safe to breathe.

Humans weren't the only ones issued with gas masks –
horses, dogs and carrier pigeons got them as well!

HOW TO SEND A MESSAGE IN SCARY CIRCUMSTANCES

Just imagine – you're stuck in a hole in the ground being bombed left, right and centre, and you're running out of ammunition. There are no mobile phones, no computers, no internet, no walkie-talkies and nobody can hear you shout over the noise of the explosions. If you don't get help soon, you'll be going home in a body bag (well, bits of you will be going home, but some of you will probably be left in the hole for the rats).

So how exactly do you send a message saying that you need help?

1) Use a human – write a note on a piece of paper and get a messenger (called a 'runner') to carry it to its destination.

Maybe not! Being a World War One runner is one of the most dangerous jobs around. Even if they run really fast, they'll be lucky not to get killed!

600-METRE MESSAGE MEDAL

In 1916 Sergeant-Major George Evans won a medal for bravery. He'd volunteered to take a message across the battlefield after five other runners had been killed attempting it. He ran across 600 metres of open ground while under fire, zigzagging and jumping from hole to hole for cover. Even though he was wounded, he made it there and back!

2) Use a dog – to avoid risking the lives of human runners, you can use a specially trained dog instead. They can run faster and are less likely to be fired on by the enemy. They're so useful that back in Britain stray dogs are being rounded up and sent to a special 'War Dog School' to be trained as messenger dogs!

3) What about flags? – send a message in code using lots of different coloured flags.

The problem with flags is that you can't see them in the dark, and in daylight any arms that are waving them are likely to get shot off.

4) A torch? – soldiers have worked out a brilliant way of sending coded messages by using flashing lights!

But if the enemy knows your code they can read your message too!

71

5) A telephone? – you may not have a mobile phone. Never mind, though, there are telephone lines all across Europe.

But in an emergency there probably won't be a telephone nearby, and if you want one installed you'll have to wait for days.

6) A radio? – radio has just been invented.

But there aren't many of them, and they're bulky, difficult to carry and only have a short range.

7) How about a pigeon?

What???

What???

A pigeon???

Yes, use a specially trained homing pigeon. They're often your best chance of sending information in the heat of battle. Not only do they have a fantastic sense of direction, but they fly so fast and high that it's difficult to shoot them down. Over 100,000 carrier pigeons were used in the war and they had a ninety-five per cent success rate!

Pigeons win!

A MEDAL-WINNING PIGEON

In 1918 a pigeon called 'Cher Ami' ('Dear Friend') carried a message asking for help from a group of American soldiers stuck behind enemy lines to their friends in the trenches. The brave little bird was shot through the breast, blinded in one eye, and by the time she'd delivered the message, one of her legs was so badly injured that it was dangling from her body by a single tendon. She was awarded a medal for saving the lives of over a hundred soldiers!

No more jobs today, s'il vous plaît. I'm feeling a bit poorly . . .

CHAPTER THREE

TWENTY THOUSAND GLASS EYES

In World War One millions of men were killed or injured. The statistics are mind-blowingly, knee-wobblingly horrible!

In 1915 nearly **2 million** Russian soldiers died or were badly hurt.

In June 1916 the Austro-Hungarian Army suffered **280,000** casualties in one week.

In August 1914 the French Army lost **211,000** men in sixteen days.

In 1916 alone the German Army lost **1.4 million** men.

On the first day of the Battle of the Somme in July 1916, **60,000** British soldiers died or were injured. This is the highest number of men killed on any single day in the history of the British Army.

By the end of the war **21 million** men had been seriously wounded.

Can't get a grip on those big numbers? Here are 1,000 crosses, which represent 1,000 dead people. If every page in this book looked like this one, and you bought 120 copies, you'd have just enough crosses for everyone killed in World War One.

Everywhere there were pools of blood, mounds of guts and piles of shattered bones. But behind the scenes thousands of doctors and nurses were doing their best to look after the wounded. And the good news is that because they got a lot of practice they became rather good at it.

Between 1914 and 1918 British doctors used 108 million bandages and 7,250 tons of cotton wool, fitted 1.5 million splints to 1.5 million broken limbs, and inserted over 20,000 artificial eyes into 20,000 eye sockets!

NO 999 IN NO-MAN'S-LAND

If you were hit by a bullet in no-man's-land your mates weren't allowed to stop and help you in case they got shot too. There were no emergency services to call and you couldn't ask your next-door neighbour to drive you to the nearest hospital. All you could do was try to crawl to safety and wait for a stretcher to come along.

The stretcher-bearers were under strict orders to look after the least badly injured first, because those were the soldiers who had the best chance of surviving. When your turn finally came, your problems still weren't over. It could take up to six hours to carry you through the mud to an ambulance!

LOTS OF BLOOD

Blood was a big problem on the battlefield. Adult humans usually have about ten pints pumping around inside them. They can lose one or two pints without too much of a problem, but if someone blows a big hole in their body, lots of blood will leak out.

It doesn't just 'leak'. If you get a really big wound in the wrong place it'll spurt out in big jets and you'll bleed to death in under a minute.

Shut up, Grace. This is a book for children, not vampires!

Can't I read it too?

Until 1917 the only way to replace lost blood was to connect a long tube to another person who had a similar blood group and take blood from their body.

Tell me more!

But this was a tricky process and relied on finding some nice person nearby who'd give you their blood at the crucial moment.

I love gorgeous people like that!

Eventually one doctor had the bright idea of collecting it in special bottles, storing the bottles in an icebox and transporting them to hospital tents near the front line, where they could be used when needed.

He'd invented the first blood bank!

Wow! That's my kind of bank!

Today all hospitals use blood banks to give them quick access to blood in an emergency!

That's enough about blood. Let's get on to the next bit.

WARNING: ACTUALLY THIS BIT IS PRETTY DISGUSTING TOO!

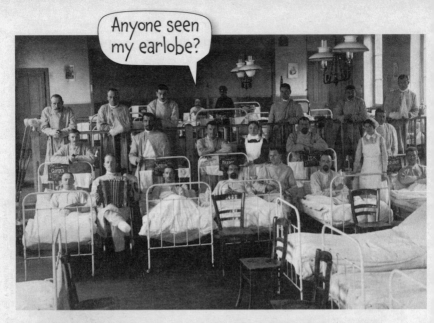

THE SHOP THAT SOLD TIN NOSES

Soldiers didn't just lose arms, legs, hands, feet and eyes; some lost their noses too.

Mirrors were often banned in hospitals in case soldiers with badly damaged faces saw their reflection and collapsed in shock. But some doctors were determined to try to put the battered faces of the injured men back together again.

Like all army doctors, surgeon Harold Gillies had a huge workload. For instance, after the first day of the Battle of the Somme he was presented with 2,000 new patients. Gradually he and his team developed ways of repairing faces, using pieces of skin from other parts of their patients' bodies to patch up their wounds and make their injuries less obvious.

But if a man's face was too badly damaged for this kind of treatment Gillies fitted a metal mask over his face which was painted to match his skin colour. Fake eyebrows, eyelashes and a moustache were then glued on to it using real hair. These masks were made in a workshop in a London hospital known as the 'Tin Noses Shop'.

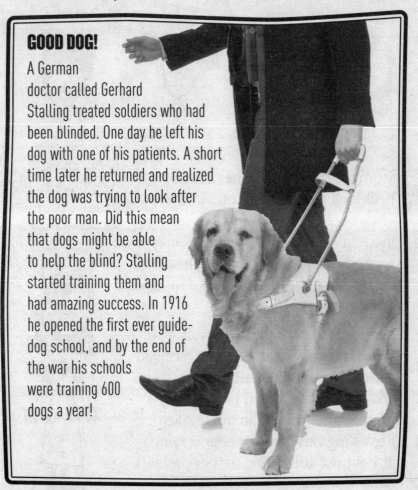

GOOD DOG!

A German doctor called Gerhard Stalling treated soldiers who had been blinded. One day he left his dog with one of his patients. A short time later he returned and realized the dog was trying to look after the poor man. Did this mean that dogs might be able to help the blind? Stalling started training them and had amazing success. In 1916 he opened the first ever guide-dog school, and by the end of the war his schools were training 600 dogs a year!

A SPECIAL TEST
FOR OUR FEMALE READERS

Girls, if you saw a severed leg on the ground would you . . .

A: Scream and pass out?

B: Throw up?

C: Tut loudly at the mess, pick it up and put it out of the way where people wouldn't trip over it?

Sensible girls and women with strong stomachs were needed to help look after the sick and injured. They became nurses and worked incredibly long hours cleaning dirty wounds, bandaging bleeding heads and helping to saw off badly damaged arms and legs.

If you chose 'C', you'd have made a great World War One nurse!

Some got awards for bravery. British aristocrat Lady 'Dot' Feilding received a medal for driving ambulances around the battlefield while being shot at, and Australian nurse Alice Ross-King was given one for staying at her post and caring for her patients while dodging falling bombs.

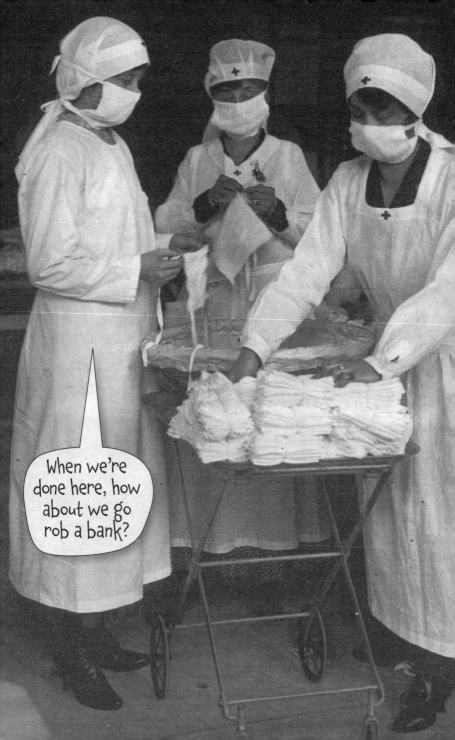

The despicable slaughter of innocent Edith Cavell by the hideously brutish, sneering, monocle-wearing, cigar-chomping, evil Boche. Note that one soldier is so ashamed of his villainy he can't bear to watch. This kind of exaggerated propaganda made a lot of Americans think that maybe they should be fighting the Germans too.

British nurse Edith Cavell is one of the great heroines of World War One. She worked for the Red Cross in Belgium, and when the Germans occupied it, she continued nursing there but at the same time secretly hid British soldiers who were trying to get back home. This was very dangerous, and when the Germans found out what she was doing, they arrested her, sentenced her to death and shot her.

But that wasn't the end of Edith's story. One of the reasons America finally joined the war was because so many Americans were outraged at the idea of a nurse being executed by a German firing squad. Her sacrifice was a big help to the Allies, even though she never knew it.

The memorial statue of Edith Cavell in London

SISSY PANTS?

Fighting in World War One was pant-wettingly, unimaginably terrifying, and many soldiers fell ill with a newly identified illness known as 'shell shock'. The horror of the dreadful things they'd experienced gave some of them weird facial tics. Others had terrifying nightmares and woke up sweating and screaming, or suddenly went blind, or couldn't eat, talk or walk.

At first doctors thought they were simply pretending in order to get away from the fighting. They were told to stop being sissy pants and to pull themselves together. Some were even shot for being cowards.

But a few wiser people said that anyone who'd been stuck in the middle of a battle surrounded by bodies, had been shot at and shelled, and had stabbed men to death with their bayonet, was highly likely to be driven a little crazy by the experience. In fact they thought

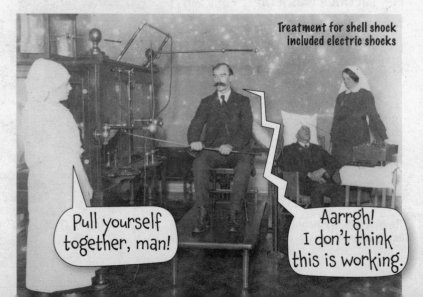

Treatment for shell shock included electric shocks

it was surprising that every single soldier in the army wasn't shell-shocked.

Almost 80,000 British soldiers ended up suffering in this way and it was very difficult to cure them. Ten years after the war finished, 65,000 men were still receiving treatment for shell shock.

ATISHOO

But weapons weren't the only killers. Disease wiped out more people than all the shells, bombs and guns put together.

For instance, flu isn't very nice, but if you stagger up to bed, moan a lot, eat grapes and watch loads of DVDs you'll usually be right as rain again in a couple of weeks. But not if you lived at the end of World War One.

In 1918 a deadly disease called Spanish Flu hit the armies of Europe. Large numbers of soldiers from all over the world were living in unhealthy conditions in the trenches. This helped spread the flu virus really quickly. Soldiers caught a terrible fever and died within days. Armies on both sides lost thousands of men.

The flu virus looks something like this (though not as big, obviously)

Spanish Flu killed over 50 million people worldwide – more than the war itself!

CHAPTER FOUR

WAR IN THE AIR AND AT SEA

World War One didn't just happen on land. There were battles in the air as well. But flying in 1914 took a lot of guts, because planes had only just been invented!

The inventors of the first aeroplane were two American bicycle fanatics called Orville and Wilbur Wright. In 1903 they made their maiden flight. Their plane flew twenty feet above the ground and stayed in the air for a staggering twelve seconds!

That's a mighty odd bike, Orville.

Maybe that doesn't sound like a big deal, but it was the start of a completely new way of fighting wars!

They were made out of wood and cotton fabric, were held together with bits of wire and could just about carry one person – maybe two at a push. Frankly they were a bit rubbish! If you flew towards the ground too fast, the force could rip your plane's wings off.

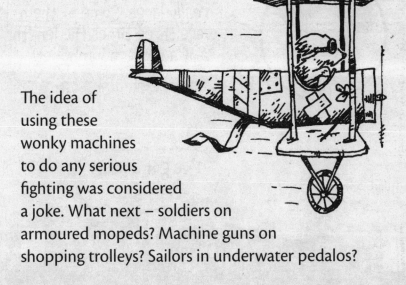

The idea of using these wonky machines to do any serious fighting was considered a joke. What next – soldiers on armoured mopeds? Machine guns on shopping trolleys? Sailors in underwater pedalos?

THE GOLDEN AGE OF AIRSHIPS

Most people thought planes were a gimmick destined for the rubbish bin of history, along with anti-fart underwear and washing machines for dogs.

Yup, somebody really invented both those things . . . if you don't believe me look them up!

Who needed 'airplanes', when you already had large pointy hot-air balloons called 'airships'?

Airships were really, really, *really* large. Some of them were three times the length of a modern jumbo jet!

I've got a nasty feeling . . .

They had engines to power them and propellers at the back for steering, with cabins underneath which could carry up to fifty passengers.

The Germans loved airships. They built some very good ones called 'Zeppelins', and when war broke out, they kitted them out for battle and sent them over to attack Britain.

On the night of 31 May 1915, a large, silent Zeppelin flew over London and began to drop bombs on the houses below, leaving seven people dead and thirty-five injured. Can you imagine how terrifying that was? Other places, including Edinburgh, Gravesend and Sunderland, were given the same treatment, and by the end of May 1916 at least 550 people had been killed.

As the war went on, new tactics were developed to defend the people on the ground. Powerful searchlights were constructed, and guns with special bullets blew the killer balloons out of the sky. By 1917 the Germans had given up using them for bombing raids, because they flew so slowly and made such an easy target. They were now a thing of the past. The future was . . . the aeroplane.

SAY CHEESE!

Even though planes were flimsy and unreliable, might they be useful on the battlefield? Could they fly over enemy territory and take photos of what was happening below?

The answer was 'yes', but these missions weren't exactly a piece of cake. Not only did you have to fly in a rickety plane low and slow over enemy positions while dodging bullets, but you also had to hold your camera steady over the side of the plane to take the pictures.

And in those days cameras weren't teeny-weeny digital things that fitted into the palm of your hand. They were big wooden boxes, and you had to slot a heavy glass plate into the box, take your picture, remove the glass plate and put a new one in . . . all without falling out of the plane!

Pilots were only given a few hours' training before they were sent up in the air. No wonder so many planes crashed or got lost! In the early years of the war more than half of all pilots died in training.

And they weren't allowed to carry parachutes in case this encouraged them to jump out of their damaged planes instead of trying to land them safely. Aeroplanes were considered more valuable than pilots. No wonder they were known as 'flying coffins'!

COVERING A COUNTRY WITH PHOTOS

But all the effort was worth it. Photographs taken from these planes showed up all sorts of interesting things, like vehicle tracks which told you where the enemy had gone, or suspicious shapes that showed where guns were hidden. They could also help you make accurate maps, which were essential if you wanted to attack the enemy in a foreign land.

Planes became stronger and faster. Cameras also improved. Eventually photos taken 15,000 feet above the ground could be enlarged to show a single footprint in the mud below!

By the end of the war millions of aerial photographs had been taken. The Germans reckoned that if all their air photos had been laid side by side they would have covered Germany *six* times over!

NO MORE MR NICE PILOT

As more and more planes took to the skies, pilots from opposite sides began to meet in mid-air. At first they just smiled and waved. Then they remembered they were supposed to be fighting a war, so they started shouting insults and making rude hand signs. Soon they were throwing bricks and grenades, and firing pistols at each other.

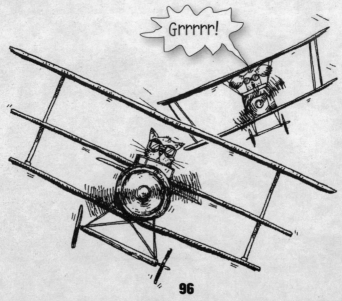

Grrrrr!

The first time a pilot brought down an enemy aircraft was in September 1914, when a Russian plane rammed an Austrian one. It wasn't a very smart thing to do: both aircraft crashed and the pilots died. But it was the start of air combat.

It wasn't long before planes were being fitted with machine guns. British pilot Louis Strange even fixed a 'safety strap' to his, so his co-pilot could stand up during the flight and fire his gun in any direction without falling out.

Two French airmen looking very silly

Serious aerial combat between
the British and Germans, 1915

Look what I won at the fair, Mum!

British observation balloon and balloon shed, 1915

BALLOON BUSTING!

Each side had enormous observation balloons suspended above the battlefield, with a soldier in a basket underneath who sent messages down to the ground. These balloons were a tempting target for aircraft, and some pilots became expert 'balloon busters', flying at them and firing bullets until they exploded. Belgian pilot Willy Coppens held the record for the number of popped enemy observation balloons: thirty-five!

Balloon busting was a dangerous game. You could be shot down by enemy guns, or your plane's wing could get caught in the wire cables hanging between them. Sometimes decoy balloons were sent up with baskets full of high explosives in them which were remotely detonated if a plane came close.

THE RED BARON

No pilot was more famous than the German Baron Manfred von Richthofen (pronounced 'Rickt-hoff-en'). He was known as the 'Red Baron', and was so confident nobody could catch him that he painted his plane bright red. He shot down a colossal eighty British planes before he was finally hit by a single bullet in April 1918 while in mid-flight. He managed to land his plane safely near the Australian trenches, but died shortly afterwards.

The Allies were very impressed by Richthofen, even though he was their deadly foe. His flower-covered body was taken to an aircraft hangar, where soldiers filed past to pay their respects, and he was given a full military funeral.

A French soldier with captured German plane

COOL PLANE!

Baron von Richthofen

COOL GUY!

PRETEND PARIS

Planes could also be used to drop bombs. In the early days of aerial warfare this simply meant flying over enemy territory and chucking one out of your aircraft in the general direction of your target. It wasn't very scientific but it could do a lot of harm.

Soon, though, aerial bombing became more efficient, and planes were developed which carried lots of bombs and could travel long distances.

They were called 'bombers'!

Eventually they were causing so much damage that the French began building an entire fake city of Paris to attract German planes away from the real Paris! They constructed pretend buildings and streets, and added realistic little details like making the windows of the pretend factories look dirty. Whether this would have fooled the Germans we'll never know, because the war ended before pretend Paris had been completed!

THIS IS PARIS. No, honest, it is.

MEANWHILE AT SEA...

In 1914 the British Navy was the best in the world. There was even a little song about it...

> Everybody sing... 'Rule Britannia, Britannia Rules the Waves... dah dah dadadada dah dah...'

Because Britain ruled the waves, it was able to seize the cargo from ships which tried to send valuable supplies to Germany.

Not only were metal, rubber and timber confiscated, but food was seized too. Soon the only coffee available in German shops was made from acorns, and the only bread was made from potatoes...

> ... with the odd bit of sawdust or chalk thrown in.

The winter of 1916 was known as the 'turnip winter', because turnips were virtually the only real food the Germans had to eat!

> You'd have been happy, Tony. You love turnips!

> No I don't – shut up, Grace!

UNDERSEA PERIL

The hungry Germans got their own back by sinking Allied ships. Enter the most feared weapon of the war – the U-boat!

By the time of World War One submarines had come a long way since the not-so-deadly 'Turtle'. German U-boats were now made of steel, could carry more than fifty crew, could stay submerged for days and were armed with guns and torpedoes. They were also silent and could sneak up to a ship, fire a torpedo and disappear again without trace. Suddenly even the biggest, most modern ships were vulnerable to attack any time of day or night. How was the Royal Navy going to defend itself?

A German U-boat, 1916

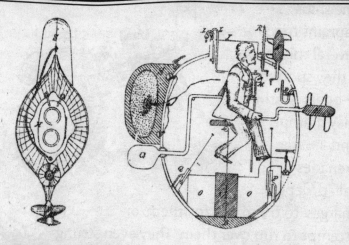

THE USELESS TURTLE

In 1776 an American inventor called David Bushnell built the 'Turtle', the world's first combat submarine. It wasn't very complicated, just a large wooden pedal-powered barrel with room for one person inside. A hole in the bottom allowed water to flow in so that it would sink, and two pumps were used to pump the water out again when you wanted to go back up to the surface. It could stay underwater for thirty minutes before the person inside the barrel ran out of air and brought the sub up . . . or failed to do so and drowned!

During the American Revolution Bushnell devised a plan to blow up a British ship in New York harbour. This involved getting the Turtle's pilot to drill a hole in the ship's bottom and then place a bomb inside. But it didn't work. The drill couldn't get through the hull. After that Bushnell tried to sink lots more British ships, but every time he failed. Eventually the British spotted the Turtle and sank it.

The ships' captains tried several things. If they spotted U-boats nearby they'd drop underwater grenades called 'depth charges' to try to destroy them, or attempt to run over them. They even strung underwater nets across the English Channel, so any U-boats that passed by would get tangled up!

But nothing seemed to work. Soon thousands of Allied ships had been sunk by killer subs. And it wasn't just warships that were under threat: all kinds of boats were attacked, including merchant vessels and even passenger liners like this one!

The luxury liner *Lusitania*

THE LUCKY CHAMPAGNE KING

In May 1915 the *Lusitania* set sail from New York bound for Liverpool. She was carrying 1,257 passengers and a crew of 702.

Despite warnings that U-boats were in the area, her passengers weren't worried. Many of them were American and their country wasn't involved in the war. And anyway the American multimillionaire Alfred Vanderbilt was on board, not to mention the so-called 'Champagne King' George Kessler, a wealthy wine salesman. The Germans wouldn't attack important people like that . . . would they?

Erm . . . well . . . yes.

The ship was travelling slowly through fog off the coast of Ireland when a U-boat commander fired a single torpedo at her. There was a thundering crack as it hit the side of the ship, which tilted sharply to the side and sank beneath the waves. 1,153 people were drowned, including Alfred Vanderbilt. (George Kessler was one of the lucky few who made it into a lifeboat.)

Mum, can I go back and get my teddy?

NOW YOU'VE DONE IT!

128 of the passengers who drowned were American. Back home their countrymen were furious! Anti-German protests broke out and Americans started muttering about teaching the Germans a lesson they'd never forget.

Even the Germans realized that sinking the *Lusitania* might have been a bad idea. They didn't need America ganging up on them as well as the Allies. So they promised to behave better in future and not to attack passenger ships.

But they didn't stick to their promise. By the beginning of 1917, German U-boats were again firing at any vessel that crossed their path. The outraged Americans declared war on Germany . . .

This was the best news the Allies could possibly have had. It was a bit like Superman announcing he was your new best friend. America had lots of everything – lots of food, lots of people, lots of steel and lots of money. And if the Allies were going to win the war, that's what they needed.

15 August 1917: American troops marching through the streets of London, watched by a welcoming crowd

CHAPTER FIVE

WAR ALL OVER THE WORLD

In countries all around the world there was heavy fighting...

... which is why it was called a world war!

There was fighting in Turkey...

The Turks controlled vast amounts of land known as the 'Ottoman Empire'. At its peak this empire had been one of the most powerful in the world, but by the time World War One broke out, it was old and weak.

The Allies thought the Ottoman Empire was completely useless and called it 'the sick man of Europe'.

So, late in 1914, the Turks decided to fight alongside the Germans. They thought Germany would win and if Turkey was on the winning side, the Ottoman Empire would become great again. But the Allies had other ideas. They were pretty confident they could make the Turks give in. So British, Australian and New Zealand troops launched a massive invasion from the sea at a place on the Turkish coast called Gallipoli.

This is going to be easy-peasy!

But it wasn't. In fact it was a massive failure.

The Allied soldiers were supposed to land on a gently sloping beach, but the current forced them north and they drifted on to a narrow strip of sand right under a towering cliff bristling with Turkish gunners.

The Allied troops were forced to dig trenches on the beach to protect themselves. These were even more of a nightmare than the French trenches, because in summer Turkey gets baking hot. Giant swarms of black flies covered the sweaty men, their food and the dead bodies which lay all around them . . . yuk!

The Turks up above blasted them with massive guns.
Soon the entire shoreline was red with the blood of the
helpless troops pinned down in their stinking trenches.
Casualties rocketed. Over half a million soldiers were
killed or injured. Reluctantly the Allies gave up and
pulled out. What a disaster!

The Allied forces have landed
in Gallipoli and are about to be
slaughtered

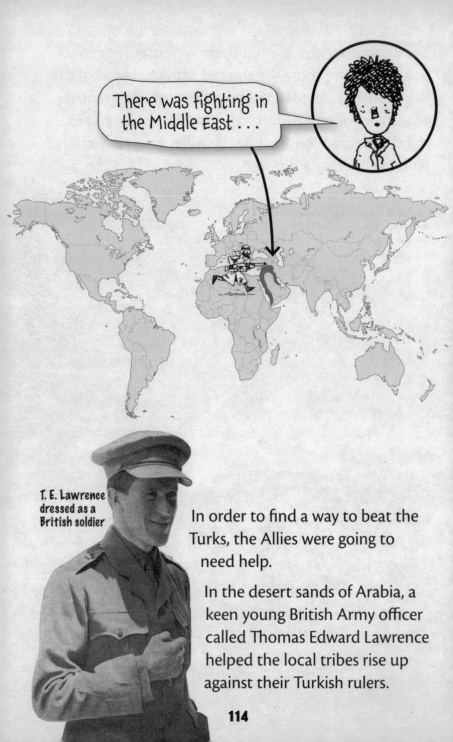

There was fighting in the Middle East . . .

T. E. Lawrence dressed as a British soldier

In order to find a way to beat the Turks, the Allies were going to need help.

In the desert sands of Arabia, a keen young British Army officer called Thomas Edward Lawrence helped the local tribes rise up against their Turkish rulers.

114

T. E. Lawrence not dressed as a British soldier

The Allies thought the Arabs weren't proper soldiers – they didn't wear uniforms or fight in a disciplined way like a European army, and they spent a lot of time arguing among themselves. But an Arab warrior had skills which were superbly useful in the desert. He could find his way through miles of sand blindfolded, could dash across sharp rocks in bare feet, and knew where to find food and water among the bone-dry sand-dunes. Not only that, but with a rifle in one hand he could jump on to a running camel and escape in the blink of an eye.

A camel? What kind of soldier wants to ride a camel?

Watch it, mate! I'm the perfect desert fighting machine, me! I can keep going for eight days without water, I've got nostrils which snap shut to keep out the sand, I'm as fast as a packhorse, as strong as an ox, I can carry tons of equipment and can travel a hundred miles a day! Oh yes, and I've got gorgeous long eyelashes! How cool am I?

At first the Arabs were suspicious of Lawrence, but they soon grew to admire him. He gave them money and guns and showed them the best way to attack the Turks, travelling deep into the desert, blowing up railway lines, bridges and telephone poles, then disappearing into the sandy wastes like a mirage. And he never seemed to get tired; he once rode his camel for 300 miles without a break!

By 1918 the Turks had lost and the Allies had seized the desert lands which had previously belonged to the Ottoman Empire. But unfortunately that didn't bring an end to the problems of the desert people who lived there. The British and French had promised to give the land back to them, but instead they greedily divided it up among themselves, crammed lots of people from different tribes together into new made-up countries like Iraq, Palestine, Jordan, Syria and Lebanon, and expected everyone to get along. Unsurprisingly this didn't work very well and lots of fights broke out which continue right up to today!

FURTHER VIOLENCE

PROTESTS IN ISRAEL

BREAKING NEWS . . . BREAKING

SYRIA: LATEST UPDATE

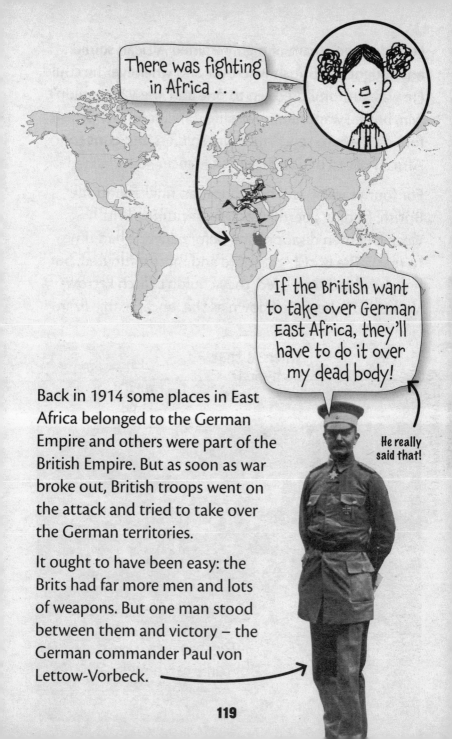

There was fighting in Africa . . .

If the British want to take over German East Africa, they'll have to do it over my dead body!

He really said that!

Back in 1914 some places in East Africa belonged to the German Empire and others were part of the British Empire. But as soon as war broke out, British troops went on the attack and tried to take over the German territories.

It ought to have been easy: the Brits had far more men and lots of weapons. But one man stood between them and victory – the German commander Paul von Lettow-Vorbeck.

He led a crack team of highly trained African soldiers and fought the British wherever and whenever he could. He was outnumbered ten to one and knew he couldn't win, but he wanted to make life difficult for the British, forcing them to send lots more soldiers and guns to Africa instead of using them in France.

For four years he and his troops ran rings round the British, leading guerrilla attacks, capturing British weapons, then disappearing before anyone had time to react. The British got more and more infuriated, but however hard they tried, they couldn't catch Lettow-Vorbeck. He became known as the 'uncatchable lizard'!

Make-up artist – my stripes are melting!

A pony disguised as a zebra for operations in East Africa

Imagine having to pull me out of your foot!

His troops were not only terrific fighters, but because they'd grown up in Africa they didn't catch all the horrible diseases that affected European soldiers. The Brits had a terrible time though. For every one of them killed in battle in Africa, another thirty died from diseases like malaria, sleeping sickness, and parasitic worms that burrowed into their bodies and feet!

The British never did catch Lettow-Vorbeck. When the war ended, the defeated Germans treated him like a hero and gave him a big parade. 120 of his men rode through the streets of Berlin, dressed in their tattered, tropical uniforms, and Lettow-Vorbeck led them, riding on a black charger.

And there was lots of fighting in Russia.

The parts of France and Belgium where the Allies and the Germans were locked in deadly combat were known as the Western Front.

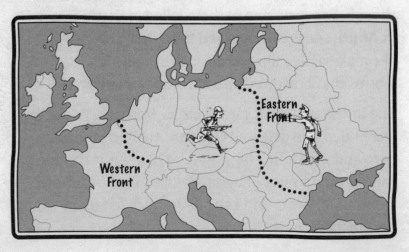

Eastern Front

Western Front

But there was an Eastern Front too. That was where the Germans were fighting the Russians.

The area over which they fought was massive. The Eastern Front was nearly 1,800 miles long, four times the size of the Western Front. The Russian army was also massive. The Russians had 6.5 million men, but only 4.5 million rifles.

HUNGRY LIKE THE WOLF

The rats in the trenches on the Western Front may have been pretty disgusting, but soldiers on the Eastern Front had to fight off hungry wolves! Matters got so bad that in the winter of 1916, German and Russian soldiers joined forces to defend themselves from crazed packs of wolves which were attacking their camps. Using poison, hand grenades and machine guns, they rounded up and killed hundreds of the fierce, furry creatures. Then they got back to killing each other.

Some Russian units were sent into battle completely unarmed and were told that if they wanted to defend themselves they'd have to take the guns from the hands of the dead bodies of the enemy. But even if they found a gun they probably wouldn't have been able to find much ammunition . . . which made winning battles just a little bit tricky. By 1916 the Russian Army had lost more than two million men!

Russian soldiers captured by the Germans in trench fighting on the Eastern Front

We may be prisoners . . .

. . . but it's much better than the snow and the wolves!

Meanwhile in Russian cities the transport systems were collapsing, prices were rising, criminals ruled the streets, and people were running out of food. Women in St Petersburg had to queue for food for forty hours a week (which is longer than most of you spend at school!).

What are we queueing for?

Bread.

A bus.

One Direction tickets.

THE LOONY MONK

The Russian ruler was Tsar Nicholas II.

Tsar, pronounced 'Zar', is Russian for Emperor.

Long hair

Craaaazy eyes

Big beard

Unfortunately for Russia, he and his wife had come under the influence of a weird, wandering holy man called Grigori Rasputin.

The Tsar and Tsarina took Rasputin's advice on how to run the country and fight the war. But the Russian people thought they were completely bonkers for listening to a mad monk, and in 1916 a group of Russian nobles invited Rasputin to dinner and murdered him.

Boy, did he take some killing!

They put poison in his pastries and in his wine, fired bullets into him, beat him with a club, and finally (just to make really sure he was dead) tied him up and dumped him in a freezing river.

Women soldiers fighting in the Russian Revolution of 1917

By 1917 the people of Russia were fed up to the back teeth with their stupid Tsar and his stupid war. In the city of St Petersburg, there was a big riot, and when the Tsar sent troops in to try and stop it, the army joined the rioters!

It was total chaos. The Tsar and his wife went into hiding and Russia pulled out of the war.

Tsar Nicholas
II, with his
family, on the
roof of Tobolsk
Prison following
the Russian
Revolution

CHAPTER SIX
THE ULTIMATE SECRET SUPER WEAPON

Meanwhile on the Western Front the opposing armies were *still* stuck in their trenches.

1918

But now, because the Russians had given in, Germany didn't have to fight on two fronts any more. Its troops swept west to smash through the Western Front and win the war once and for all.

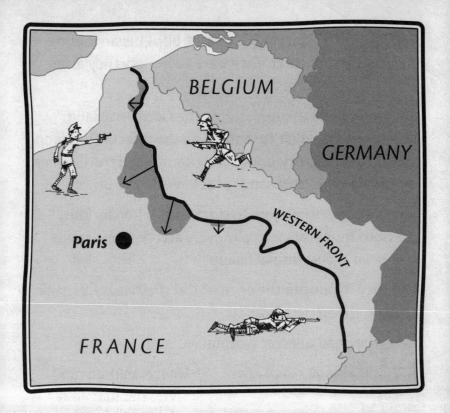

They launched a series of deadly attacks, broke through the Allied defences and continued their advance at top speed. Germany was now so confident it was going to win the war that on 24 March the Kaiser declared a national holiday!

But he'd made a big mistake. Very soon the Germans had used up all their food and ammunition, and the trucks carrying fresh supplies and weapons couldn't get through to the advancing soldiers.

Things quickly went pear-shaped.

Exhausted and starving German troops began looting Allied stores for food. They were so hungry they even ate their own horses.

The Allies had retreated during the German assault, but now it was their turn to go on the attack. They won victory after victory, completely hammered the German army and killed thousands of soldiers in the process.

So how come they were so successful, when for the previous four years virtually every attack they'd made had been such a dismal failure?

Did they hypnotize the enemy? Did they weave a magic spell on them?

No – they had a secret weapon.

German storm troops defend a series of shallow holes in the mud

What's that coming over the hill? Is it a horse? Great, I'm starving!

THE BATTLE OF AMIENS – THE BEGINNING

On 8 August 1918, at a place called Amiens in northern France, a massive force of Allied troops prepared to attack the German trenches.

Over the previous four years there had been hundreds of similar attacks, but thick barbed wire, deep trenches and lines of machine guns had made it almost impossible to break through.

This attack would be different though.

No guns were fired until the moment the battle began (which meant the enemy wasn't ready for an attack)!

Lots of bombs were dropped to soften up the enemy.

The army wasn't sent in first . . .

Instead, in the early-morning mist, the terrifying rumbling of the new super weapon echoed across the fields of Amiens.

Very poetic, Jojo!

Thanks!

The Allies' new secret super weapon was ... **tanks**!
Their massive size and enormous treads allowed them
to smash through barbed wire, roll over trenches
and demolish machine-gun positions with a metallic
crunching noise.

THE LIGHT-BULB MOMENT

And how had British boffins come up with the idea of
inventing such a terrifying new weapon?

The answer is ... tractors!

Yes, folks, we were
the inspiration!

From early in the war, tractors with caterpillar treads were used to haul big guns around the battlefield. They were perfect for the job because they were the only vehicles that didn't get stuck in muddy ground.

So ... PING!

How about building a bulletproof tractor with a gun on the front?

This was a genuine light-bulb moment!

The British secretly began work on an armour-plated, tractory-gunny, German-squishing super machine, which at first they called the 'Landship'. But they soon changed its name ...

It doesn't look like an armour-plated, tractory-gunny, German-squishing super machine at all. It looks like something to keep water in.

Hmmm! Wouldn't it be a good idea if the Germans thought we were trying to invent something to keep water in rather than an armour-plated, tractory-gunny, German-squishing super machine?

Yes, an excellent idea! Let's call it the 'Thing to Keep Water In'.

That's rubbish!

What about the 'Water Cistern'?
Oh, come on!
Errr . . . the 'Water Tank'?
Who said that? Brilliant idea! We'll call it the 'Tank'!
The tank! The tank! The flippin' tank!!!

The first tank rolled off the production line on
8 September 1916 – Hooray!

Two days later its tracks fell off – Boo!

But the British repaired it – Hooray!

And it broke down again – Boo!

Making a reliable tank wasn't going to be easy.

Tanks were first used in battle in 1916. But most of
them broke down repeatedly. If they were driven over
swampy ground they sank, and even on good ground
they were really slow.

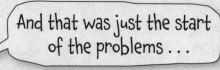

And that was just the start of the problems . . .

A tank needed lots of people to make it work – a driver, someone to work the brakes, two people to change the gears and four to fire the guns.

The engine was situated right next to the crew-members, making everything noisy, hot and cramped.

In battle every hatch, flap and door was shut to protect it from attack. But this meant that the people inside could pass out, because the fumes from the engine were so lethal.

And it was pitch black inside your tank, so you had to learn how to drive it by touch alone.

And to cap it all, tanks were massively vulnerable to attack. They made easy targets because they were so big and slow, and if one was hit by a shell it could burst into flames.

And as they only had tiny escape hatches crews sometimes got trapped inside and burned to death.

MY GANG'S BIGGER THAN YOUR GANG

When the Germans finally realized what the Allies were up to, they tried to develop tanks too . . . but it was too late. By the end of the war the British and French had built over 5,000, while the Germans had only twenty!

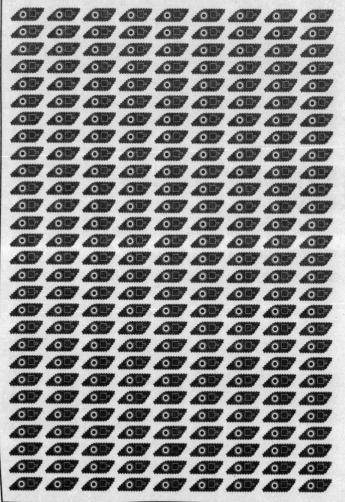

THE BATTLE OF AMIENS – THE END

Eventually, by 1918, the boffins had made lots of improvements, they'd cracked most of the technical problems, and the Allies finally had enough reliable

tanks to launch an effective attack. At Amiens 580 of them led the way. They broke through the enemy lines and advanced so quickly that one party of German officers was captured while they were still eating their breakfast!

On that first day of battle the Allies advanced over seven miles, taking 17,000 German prisoners and killing or wounding 30,000 more! It became known as the 'Black Day of the German Army'. Imagine how excited the Allies were – suddenly an end to the agony of trench warfare seemed possible! With tanks and aircraft they might just win the war and finally be able to go home!

BREAKING THE HINDENBURG LINE

But not just yet.

There was still one big problem –
the 'Hindenburg Line'...

... named after the man who ordered it to be built, the head of the German army, Paul von Hindenburg.

It was a network of deep concrete trenches up to
fifteen feet deep and twelve feet wide, surrounded
by a wall of barbed wire sixty feet thick, with
a 'battle zone' of over a mile in front of it
guarded by machine guns and artillery.

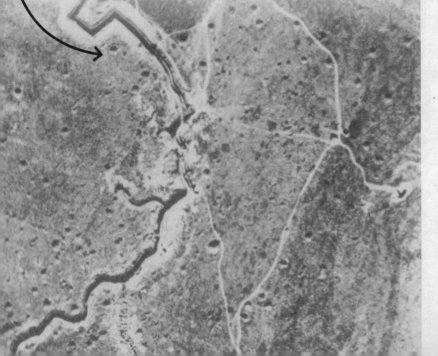

British, Australian, French and American forces launched an attack on it. They used their big guns first to try to smash it. Then tanks and aircraft supported the soldiers as they advanced against the concrete trenches. On 29 September they finally broke through! The Germans were beaten. Within days they surrendered. The Allies had won!

France, 1918: all that's left here is destruction

Sgt. J. W. Milner. Pte. G. E. Ellison. Pte. H. Jubb.

THE UNLUCKIEST MAN

Perhaps the unluckiest man in the whole war was George Edwin Ellison. He'd been fighting since 1914 and had lived through some pretty hairy battles, but was shot dead by the enemy while on patrol just an hour and a half before the war ended.

WHAT HAPPENED NEXT?

The war had cost billions and billions of pounds. Millions had lost their lives. The world would never be the same again.

Most soldiers went home and tried to forget about all the horrible things they'd seen and done.

GRANDPA JACK

BABY ME

My Grandpa Jack came back to London from the trenches in 1918, threw his uniform on the sitting-room fire, watched it burn and never spoke about the war ever again.

Over the next few years people kicked out lots of the kings and emperors who'd dragged their country into this stupid war, and tried to make sure that in future they'd be ruled by ordinary folk instead.

THE UNLUCKIEST COW

So many bombs and mines were used in World War One that a few still pose a danger today. Some years ago a bolt of lightning set off an old World War One mine in Belgium and killed a cow!

Old and mighty empires like the Ottoman Empire and the Austro-Hungarian Empire collapsed, and the Russians got rid of Tsar Nicholas. He was executed along with his family in July 1918.

Kaiser Wilhelm of Germany was booted out too, but lots of Germans were still very angry. They thought they should have won, and sincerely believed they would have done so if they'd been allowed to keep on fighting.

Just twenty years later Germany was ready to fight again, and this time an even bigger and deadlier war broke out.

But that's another story . . .

TIMELINE

28 Jun 1914 The Austro-Hungarian nobleman Archduke Franz Ferdinand is assassinated in Sarajevo

Aug 1914 War is declared

Sep 1914 The armies dig into their trenches

1915 Allied soldiers are machine-gunned on the beach at Gallipoli

22 Apr 1915 The Germans start using chlorine gas on their enemies

7 May 1915 British passenger ship the *Lusitania* is attacked by a German submarine and sinks. Over 1,000 passengers die, including some Americans – and America considers joining the war

31 May 1915 A German airship flies over London to drop bombs

1916 The world's first school for guide dogs for the blind opens in Germany

1 Jul 1916 The Battle of the Somme begins, after British shells fail to scare the Germans off. 60,000 British soldiers are killed or injured on a single day

Sep 1916 The British start using tanks in battle (but they're not very good yet)

Winter 1916	Germany's 'turnip winter' – so called because there was nothing else to eat
1917	The first blood bank is set up to help save wounded soldiers
Jan 1917	A huge blast destroys an explosives factory in London – along with 900 of its neighbours' houses!
Feb 1917	The Russians have a revolution and kick out their Tsar
6 Apr 1917	America joins in the war, on the side of the Allies
Nov 1917	Russia has another revolution and leaves the war
Apr 1918	The German air ace Baron von Richthofen is shot down and killed, having brought down eighty British planes during the war
Jun 1918	The Spanish Flu epidemic hits Europe and kills even more people than the war
8 Aug 1918	Hundreds of new, improved tanks make their appearance at the Battle of Amiens
Sep 1918	The Allies break through the Hindenburg Line and the Germans have to give in
Oct 1918	Carrier pigeon Cher Ami saves the lives of nearly 200 American soldiers on her last mission
11 Nov 1918	Germany and the Allies sign the armistice – an agreement that the war is officially over

QUIZ

"YOUR COUNTRY NEEDS **YOU**"

1 Who killed Archduke Franz Ferdinand?
- the Black Hand Gang
- the Blue Nose Gang
- the Green Finger Gang

2 How many grandchildren did Queen Victoria have?

3 Who was the man on the 'Your Country Needs You' poster?

4 What did all members of the British Army have to grow in 1914?
- prize marrows
- Mohican hairdos
- moustaches

5 What do you call a spade if it's not a spade?

6 How did the French get emergency soldiers to the Front in 1914?

7 What shape were trenches built in?

8 What was the British royal family's surname before it was Windsor?

9 What were the women who worked in explosives factories called?

10 Which deadly weapon was invented by Hiram Maxim in the 1880s?

11 Why would soldiers wee on their own socks?

12 What were the big balloons called that were used before aeroplanes?

13 Why weren't pilots allowed to carry parachutes?
- because they were too heavy
- so they wouldn't jump out and waste a precious plane
- in case they didn't work

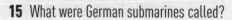

14 What was the colourful nickname of Baron Manfred von Richthofen?

15 What were German submarines called?

16 Who was 'the sick man of Europe'?

17 Where did T. E. Lawrence give money and guns to the locals?

18 Which terrifying animals were a danger to soldiers on the Eastern Front?

19 Which vehicle gave British boffins the idea for an armoured tank?

20 Which line did the Allies have to cross to win the war?

WORLD WAR II

To my friend Jessica Cobb, who does the research for the Weird World of Wonders books. She's just about to have a baby girl, who will probably be as clever as she is. This is great for me, because by the time the baby's two she's bound to be able to read and write, and I'll get her to do all my research instead of Jess; and I won't have to pay her, I'll just give her penny sweets and little cartons of juice. It'll save me loads of money! Thanks, Jess.

To Mum and Dad Not many of us know what it's like to be in a war, particularly one that could end with our country being taken over by a cruel and racist dictator. But my mum and dad's generation spent six years of their lives in the fight against Hitler, and if it wasn't for them Britain would be a horrible place to live in. We owe them a huge debt of gratitude. So thanks Mum, thanks Dad, and sorry I was a little monster sometimes.

Hello, again!

Now we come to wheelbarrows full of
money and things that go bang.
Read about friends and enemies, and standing up to
bullies – and also moustaches, secret codes and
plenty more besides!

Turn the page to find out . . .

INTRODUCTION

BOOM!

BOOM!

In 1914 the biggest war ever broke out across the world – millions of people were killed or injured.

BOOM!

It was a war so big it was called **'The Great War'.**

. . . And it dragged on for four muddy, bloody and brutal years. When it finally ended everyone breathed a huge sigh of relief, safe in the knowledge that nothing so horrible would be allowed to happen ever again.

Phew!!!

Everyone went back to their everyday lives.

Films, which until then had been silent and in black-and-white, now had sound and colour!

Girls cut their hair into bobs, wore short flappy dresses, and did a crazy dance called the Charleston.

People drove cars and travelled by plane, and visited places they'd never been to before.

Inventors came up with thousands of crazy inventions like the ballpoint pen and the chocolate chip cookie.

Jazz records sold by the thousand and went to the top of the charts.

Then suddenly . . . *EVERYBODY DUCK!*

. . . this happened.

Germany invaded Poland.

It happened at 4.40 a.m. on 1 September 1939 while most people were still tucked up in bed asleep. Planes appeared overhead and started dropping bombs. (The Poles soon woke up – there's nothing like earth-shattering explosions to get you going in the morning.) More than a million German soldiers flooded across the Polish border, armed with a frightening array of state-of-the-art weapons and supported by tanks and aircraft. The Germans called this attack . . .

Nobody had ever seen anything like it!

Blitzkrieg means 'lightning war'.

They moved lightning-fast, capturing towns and cities, executing anyone who stood in their way. Wave after wave of planes destroyed railways and roads, and gunned down people who tried to run off. There was total chaos.

'Oi,' said Britain and France, 'this is no way to behave! Back off!' And they declared war on Germany.

World War Two had begun, and it would turn out to be even bigger and deadlier than the Great War.

In fact it was the biggest and deadliest war in history!

That's really something because there'd been loads of wars before.

Yeah, between Stone Age tribes, between ancient empires, between great kingdoms . . .

Some, like the Hundred Years War, went on for ages.

One, called the Anglo-Zanzibar war, only lasted 38 minutes!

World War Two involved 61 countries and more than 100 million fighting men! It went on for six years and by the time it was over a colossal 70 million people had died.

So what was it all about? Why did Germany invade Poland, and what happened next?

CHAPTER ONE
THE WEIRDO WITH A GLEAM IN HIS EYES

So what made the Germans start World War Two? It's not like they just woke up one morning and said to one another, 'Hey, I've got a really crazy idea. Let's invade Poland!'

Guess which one of these blokes will soon become a megalomaniac dictator?

HITLER THE CRY BABY

Among the thousands of German men who had fought in World War One was a weirdly weird weirdo with a crazy gleam in his eyes. His name was Adolf Hitler.

He loved being a soldier. He used to volunteer for all the mad, dangerous jobs like running between the trenches with messages while dodging falling bombs. Several times he narrowly escaped being blown to bits.

He won lots of medals for bravery, but his fellow soldiers, who were fed up with the rotten food, the muddy trenches and being shot at every day, thought he was a nutter. They fancied going home, but Adolf told them that anyone who wanted to bottle out was a traitor.

When his beloved Germany finally surrendered, Hitler was gutted. In fact he was so upset he cried for days.

It had all started twenty years earlier at the end of the Great War. The Germans had lost, and they weren't at all happy about it. The trouble was that the countries which won (like America, Britain and France) wanted them to pay for all the damage that had been done (which was A LOT – the total bill came to £22,000,000,000. War isn't cheap!).

The Germans were bewildered and angry. They had thought they were going to win. They HAD been winning in the beginning. And now they were supposed to pay back all this money. How unfair can you get!

THE WHOLE WORLD GETS DEPRESSED

While the Germans were moaning about how badly they were being treated, everyone else was busy celebrating the end of the war, spending money on jazz records, cars, and chocolate chip cookies.

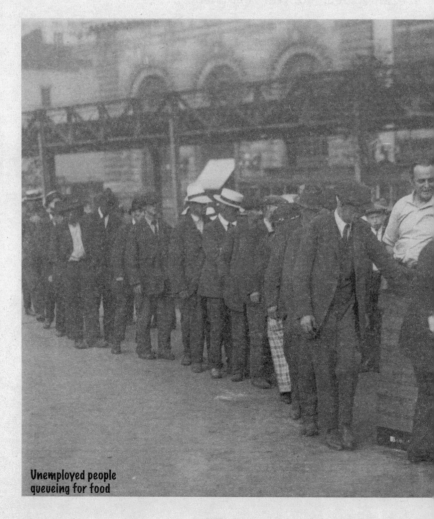

Unemployed people queueing for food

This dreadful time was called the 'Great Depression'.

That was a good name for it!

But then suddenly in 1929 the whole world went bust! Banks and businesses closed, people lost their jobs because there was no money to pay their wages, and families couldn't afford food or heating.

Life may have been bad everywhere else, but in Germany, they had to pay off their colossal debt too. For ordinary Germans things were truly desperate!

MONEY IN A WHEELBARROW

Imagine if you had a machine that could print money – just think of all the things you could buy!

1,642 pairs of trainers!

The entire Manchester United First Team . . . plus the reserves!

A bone the size of the Isle of Wight!

But believe it or not, it's possible to have too much of the stuff. In Germany in the early 1920s, the government printed more and more paper notes to try and make up for the lack of money.

Soon there were banknotes everywhere! So many were printed that they became almost worthless. You had to fill a wheelbarrow with banknotes to buy a loaf of bread!

Sometimes a robber would nick the wheelbarrow and leave the money on the ground because it wasn't worth anything. Lots of people gave the contents of their wallets to their children to play with, or made kites out of all the different-coloured notes!

What could the Germans do to get out of this mess?
They didn't have anything to eat and the future looked
grim.

The politicians weren't any help. They just argued with
each other all the time. People thought they needed
somebody to sort things out for them – someone who
could make Germany rich and successful again . . .

The German Emperor and Hitler

NASTY NAZIS

By now Hitler was the leader of a bunch of people
called the 'Nationalist Socialist German Workers Party'
(or 'Nazis' for short) who were all very upset about
losing the war. Hitler said Germany would have won
if CERTAIN PEOPLE hadn't sabotaged the war effort.
And if Germany hadn't lost the war, the German people
wouldn't have owed 22 billion pounds. And if they
didn't owe 22 billion pounds they'd be rich and happy.
And who do you think the CERTAIN PEOPLE were that
Hitler was on about?

The Army Generals . . . for coming up with terrible
battle plans and sending soldiers to their deaths?

The Politicians . . . for starting the war in the first place
but not giving the soldiers enough weapons?

The German soldiers . . . for losing the will to fight and
not being able to beat the enemy?

The Jews . . . for, um . . . being Jewish?

The answer is – he blamed them all . . .
but particularly the Jews!

Let's face it –
he was stupid
and crazy!

I BLAME THE JEWS BECAUSE I'M DUMB

The Jewish religion has been around for thousands of years; it's even older than other big religions like Christianity and Islam.

Lots of Jews have special customs like going to synagogue (a place of worship), wearing symbolic clothing (like a little cap called a 'Kippah'), living together in one community, and speaking a special language called Hebrew.

All in all, pretty harmless stuff. Yet throughout history Jewish people have been blamed when things go wrong.

Why?

It's probably because people can be stupid and often like blaming other folk for their problems, and as Jews are often seen as 'different', they're an easy target.

I said put your Kippah on!

Hands up if you think I'm great.

Hitler at a Nazi rally

Hitler made rabble-rousing speeches about what the Jews had done to his beloved country. He ranted and raved, rocked from side to side, his eyes bulging, his hands waving, his voice getting louder and louder, and with sweat pouring off him.

He was as mad as a box of frogs but he was very good at making speeches, and people grew to believe he could make Germany great again. By 1933 the Nazi Party had 800,000 members, and Hitler was so popular he was made the ruler of Germany!

HEIL HITLER!

The Nazi Party became Hitler's own army. Its members wore special military-style uniforms, and had badges with special crosses on them called 'swastikas'.

Nazis marched about swinging their arms and legs (this was called 'goose-stepping'), and used a special salute, shooting their right arm straight up in the air and shouting 'Heil Hitler!'

Mum, I don't want to do that. It's stupid.

177

A Jewish shop, smashed by the Nazis

It looked pretty daft but you didn't want to laugh at the Nazis (at least not to their faces), because if you did, they'd beat you up. They thumped anyone they didn't like. After Hitler became leader, they marched through the cities of Germany beating up Jews and setting fire to their synagogues.

Mind you, they did stop goose-stepping after a while, because they couldn't do it properly!

I can, and it still looks stupid!

THINGS JEWISH PEOPLE WERE NOT ALLOWED TO DO IN NAZI GERMANY

As soon as they came to power, the Nazis started introducing lots of laws that banned Jewish people from doing certain things, like:

- Marrying anyone who wasn't Jewish
- Teaching
- Working for the government
- Being a lawyer or a doctor
- Playing in public parks
- Travelling on buses and trains
- Driving
- Renting a house
- Going to school
- Owning a business
- Swimming in public swimming pools
- Being German!

THINGS THAT JEWISH PEOPLE WERE ALLOWED TO DO IN NAZI GERMANY

Ermmm . . .

- . . . Just about nothing!

Across Germany, people started believing all this anti-Jewish nonsense. They refused to talk to their Jewish neighbours, stopped buying food from shops owned by Jews, fired their Jewish employees, and told their kids they weren't allowed to be friends with Jewish kids.

By 1933, if you were a Jew in Germany you thought seriously about moving somewhere like America or Switzerland . . . in fact anywhere that wasn't Germany. Thousands packed their bags and left home to find a new life. But not everyone could afford to leave. For those who stayed, life got worse and worse.

Jews had to wear a star on their clothes – even when they were doing PE

SPREADING THE HATE

It wasn't just Jews who suffered. Hitler hated gypsies, foreigners, gay and black people; he called them 'sub-human'. He made this word up because he wanted Germans to believe they weren't proper people.

TEENAGE NAZIS

Even kids were allowed to be Nazis. Hitler created a special club called the 'Hitler Youth' for young people between the ages of ten and eighteen. He was a loony but he wasn't stupid. He knew that lots of kids believe in daft things, and that if they joined his 'club' it would be easy to brainwash them into believing anything he said. Then, when they grew up, they'd be Nazis too.

He could also use them as little spies. They were ordered to keep an eye on their parents and report them to the Nazis if they did anything suspicious. One boy called Walter Hess told them that his dad had said Hitler was a crazed lunatic. The Nazis promptly came round, marched his dad away and locked him up!

In the Hitler Youth, boys were taught how to be soldiers. They practised marching, shooting, trench digging and throwing grenades. It was all part of Hitler's big plan.

Girls were taught cooking, cleaning and bed-making. There was also the odd bit of pistol-shooting thrown in . . . because if there was ever another war, it would be useful if girls could shoot!

And don't think you could make excuses to get out of the Hitler Youth like 'I can't do marching, I've got a verruca!' A law was passed saying every kid had to join (unless they were Jewish, obviously!).

HITLER'S CRAZY PLAN

Hitler's plan was to turn the Germans into a super-race of blond-haired, blue-eyed, muscle-bound warriors.

He wanted them to take over the whole world, so he could rule it with an iron fist.

To do that, he decided to wipe out the weak, the dirty, the old, the sick and anyone who stood in his way.

Ha Ha!

Ha Ha! Ha Ha!

Ha Ha Ha Haaa! Ha Ha Ha Ha Haaa! Ha Ha Ha Ha Haaa!

Oh, do shut up!

Of course, he couldn't just come out and say this, because other countries might try to stop him. He had to move quietly and step-by-step.

1 The first step was to take control of Germany.

2 The second was to get rid of anyone who was 'different', like Jews, and gypsies, or the old and sick. Nazi doctors started quietly killing off people with disabilities.

3 The third step was to invade the next-door countries, get rid of the people who lived there, and replace them with superman-type Germans . . .

In 1938 his troops marched into neighbouring Austria and took it over. This made Britain and France very uneasy, but Austria didn't seem to mind much, and nobody wanted another big war, so they kept quiet . . .

Then Hitler demanded to be given part of a country called Czechoslovakia. This time there was a bit more muttering from the French and British. They really didn't like the way things were going at all.

Hitler promised that there was nothing to worry about – he said that once he'd taken a teensy bit of Czechoslovakia he'd be happy and wouldn't invade anywhere else. And almost everybody believed him!

Then he invaded the rest of Czechoslovakia. Now Britain and France felt really stupid.

Finally, in September 1939, Hitler ordered the invasion of Poland.

At last Britain and France had had enough. This meant

WAR!

CHAPTER TWO
THE CHARGING RHINO

Within days, more than 150,000 British soldiers had been sent across the Channel and into France – the British and French armies were going to sort Hitler out. With any luck, they'd be back in time for tea...

Unfortunately, stopping Hitler was easier said than done. It was like trying to step in front of a charging rhino. Four weeks after his army invaded Poland, the entire country was under German and Russian control.

Then, before the British and French armies could stop them, the Germans had torn through Belgium...

. . . and Holland . . .

. . . and into northern France.

Once again German planes bombed everything and everybody, while tanks and soldiers poured across the borders and took control of France's towns and cities.

Under this terrifying pressure the French army collapsed, and the Brits retreated in order to avoid being wiped out, leaving most of their weapons and kit behind!

THE GREAT ESCAPE

By the end of May 1940, hundreds of thousands of British and French soldiers were trapped on the French coast in a seaside resort called Dunkirk. The German forces were all around them; German bombs rained down on them, and all the Brits could do was sit on the beach and hope they'd be rescued.

The British government had a big problem. It only had enough boats to rescue about 30,000 men, and there were more than ten times that many on the beaches! What could be done?

A call for help was broadcast on the radio – 'Please will everyone who has a boat, even a small one, lend it to us so we can rescue our lads.' People responded in their hundreds. Fleets of little rowing boats, fishing boats, sailing yachts and bath tubs (well, maybe not) bobbed across the English Channel to pick up the soldiers on the French beaches.

More than 338,000 men were rescued and brought safely back to Britain. It may have been a defeat, but it felt like a victory!

British soldiers queue up to be rescued from Dunkirk

HURRICANE HEINZ!

The German tanks were called 'Panzers', which means 'armour'.

In Germany a rhinoceros like me is called a Panzernashorn!

In the UK a rhinoceros like you is called a Big Twit!

They made a terrifying noise. Their guns boomed, their engines roared, their tank tracks clanked and clattered. It was impossible to tell when the enemy was firing because the tanks always made such an ear-splitting din!

The man in charge of the Panzers was Heinz Guderian, but because his tanks moved so fast, flattening everything that stood in their way, he was known as 'Hurricane Heinz'.

THE BATTLE FOR BRITAIN

The Germans were over the moon. They'd already beaten Poland, Holland, Belgium, Denmark, Norway and France. It was like they were playing football and were 10-nil up after twenty minutes. Now was the time to prepare for the invasion of Britain.

Hitler decided to land 160,000 men in boats along the coast of England. The German soldiers assembled and waited for their instructions. It looked like the British were about to be on the receiving end of a terrible thrashing. Some people thought they should give up right away and start practising the goose-step. Those people had never met Winston Churchill.

We shall fight on the beaches, we shall fight on the landing grounds, we shall fight in the fields and in the streets, we shall fight in the hills; we shall never surrender!

Hitler wasn't the only leader with the gift of the gab. Winston Churchill was the Prime Minister of Britain, and he wowed the British people with his speeches. He was a large, funny-looking man who wore a bowler hat and smoked a big cigar. The Russians called him the 'British Bulldog' because he was so strong and stubborn.

Churchill thought Britain and its Empire were the best things since sliced bread and chocolate spread, and he had no intention of letting Hitler and his army stomp all over them. He'd always enjoyed a good battle. When he was a boy, he used to spend hours playing with thousands of toy soldiers on his nursery floor.

Later when he grew up he joined the army. He was shot at in Cuba, rode a horse in India, fought in the Sudan and was captured and escaped in South Africa. In World War One he was put in charge of the British Navy, and later led a battalion of soldiers on the Western Front. If Hitler wanted a fight, the 'British Bulldog' knew how to give him one.

Have you seen a bull? You wouldn't mess with a dog that could win a fight with one of those fierce things, would you?

Before Hitler could launch his invasion, he needed to be able to control the skies, otherwise British planes would bomb his ships as they sailed across the sea towards the south coast of Britain. So he ordered the German Air Force to attack and destroy all the RAF's planes and blow up its aerodromes and runways. But Churchill was determined that this wouldn't happen.

For the next two months German and British planes fought each other for control of the skies. This huge air battle became known as 'The Battle of Britain'.

AIR WARS

Planes were a pretty new idea. A few had been used in World War One, but back then they'd been made of bits of fabric and wood held together with glue. They were so rickety that sometimes they fell apart in mid-flight. But by 1939 Britain's planes had been given a serious upgrade. They were now made out of metal, were faster and stronger, and had gadgets like radios and heavy machine guns.

Both sides had two main types of plane:

'**Bombers**' (like the British 'Wellington' and the German 'Heinkel 177'), which were big and slow and were built to carry and drop bombs . . .

and '**Fighters**' (like the German 'Messerschmitt 109' and the British 'Spitfire' and 'Hurricane'), which were small and zippy.

Being a pilot in World War Two was no picnic – imagine climbing into a small metal box, which then shoots up thousands of metres into the air. You travel at more than 300 mph, the noise is deafening, and in front of you are a million dials and switches which never stop rattling, and which you have to watch really carefully to make sure your box doesn't fall out of the sky.

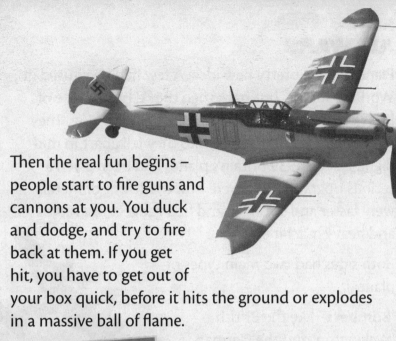

Then the real fun begins – people start to fire guns and cannons at you. You duck and dodge, and try to fire back at them. If you get hit, you have to get out of your box quick, before it hits the ground or explodes in a massive ball of flame.

"NEVER WAS SO MUCH OWED BY SO MANY TO SO FEW" THE PRIME MINISTER

HEROES OR ZEROS?

Fighter pilots who shot down more than five enemy planes were known as 'Aces' (or 'Experten' in Germany) and became heroes back home. Some got a bit carried away and said they'd shot down more planes than they really had. By the end of the war, Luftwaffe pilots claimed to have destroyed 3,058 British planes. But that can't have been true because the RAF never had that many!

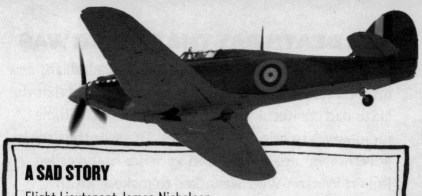

A SAD STORY

Flight Lieutenant James Nicholson
was a British fighter pilot. In August 1940 he fought a duel with
a German Messerschmitt. He was shot in the head, half blinded,
and his Hurricane caught fire. Just as he was about to jump out,
another enemy plane flew past him, so he stayed in his burning
plane, flew after it and shot it down. Only then did he bale out,
but as his parachute drifted to earth, yet another German plane
flew by and he had to pretend to be dead so it wouldn't machine-
gun him. To make things worse, before he landed, he was fired
on by the British, who thought he was a German.

Later he was given the 'Victoria Cross', the highest award for
bravery in battle. Sadly, he died shortly before the end of the war
after his plane crashed in the Bay of Bengal.

If you jump out you'll be left thousands of metres up,
plummeting towards the earth with the wind whistling
past your ears, wondering why you ever got into the
stupid box in the first place. Then, if your parachute
opens and you land without breaking both your legs,
you'll get to do the whole thing in another box the next
day. Lucky you!

THE DEATH RAY THAT NEVER WAS

One thing that really helped the RAF was a brilliant new invention. Before the war, rumours went round that the Nazis had created a 'Death Ray' which used invisible radio waves to bring down planes! This sent the British government into a panic, and a science boffin called Robert Watson-Watt was asked to make a British Death Ray.

After lots of experimenting, he decided it was impossible (it later turned out the Germans never made one either), but instead he came up with something else: a plane-detection system that used radio waves to spot planes coming even if they were a couple of hundred miles away.

Did he call it 'The Watson-Watt Plane-Detection System'?

Or 'The Magic Eye'?

It may not have been a 'Death Ray' but it was a brilliant invention.

Or 'The-Machine-For-Spotting-Enemy-Planes-From-A-Long-Way-Away'?

No, he called it 'radar' . . .

Even I knew that!

DON'T PANIC!

While the Royal Air Force was fighting the Luftwaffe in the skies, the rest of Britain was preparing for a possible invasion from the sea.

The last time we'd been successfully invaded had been by William the Conqueror in 1066. This time we'd be ready!

All round the British coast, beaches were planted with mines and covered in tangled twists of barbed wire. Miles of steel scaffolding were erected in the shallow water, and giant blocks of concrete were scattered hither and thither to get in the way of any German landing craft or tanks.

Thousands of small concrete forts called 'pillboxes' (because their shape was a bit like a giant box for pills) were put up to guard beaches, roads and rivers; and to prevent the enemy spotting them from the air and bombing them, they were sometimes disguised to look like ice-cream kiosks, haystacks and bus shelters!

Any big open spaces were covered with old cars, buses and iron bedsteads so enemy gliders couldn't land on them. Road signs were taken down, station names were painted out and petrol pumps destroyed, all in the hope that the Nazis would get lost and run out of fuel!

And people were given posters and booklets telling them what to do if there was an invasion – with helpful advice like 'Don't Panic'.

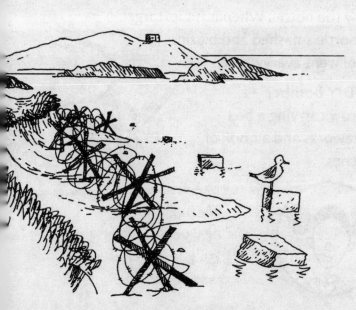

GOLF CLUBS TO THE RESCUE

To help defend the country, the government asked for part-time volunteers. One and a half million men signed up! They became known as the 'Home Guard'. At first they didn't have uniforms, and because they had so few weapons, they armed themselves with shotguns, truncheons, pickaxes, pitchforks and even golf clubs. Some members of the Home Guard even broke into museums and nicked the weapons on display! Others simply made their own. For example:

☐ **The DIY pike** – a knife welded on to the end of a piece of gas pipe.

☐ **The DIY grenade** (or 'Molotov Cocktail') – a glass bottle filled with petrol, with a bit of cloth stuck in the neck. The cloth was set alight and someone threw the bottle. When it hit its target, the bottle smashed and blazing petrol went everywhere.

☐ **The DIY bomber** – a sparrow carrying a box of fireworks and a book of matches.

Actually this one isn't true!

Another common Home Guard weapon was the **'sticky bomb'**, which was a glass globe wrapped in a glue-like covering containing high explosive. When it was thrown, it 'stuck' to its target and then exploded. The problem was that if you weren't very good at throwing, it stuck to other things – like your clothes! Aaaargh!

This one is true, and it was a pretty disgusting weapon.

A roadblock erected by the Home Guard

Women preparing for an invasion
with walking sticks and umbrellas

When you couldn't get hold of a real weapon, a pretend one would do. People were encouraged to put suspicious-looking containers in the road with bits of wire dangling from them, so passing Germans would think they were bombs and would slow down.

You were even encouraged to prop open a window of your house and stick a bit of pipe out of it, so it would look as though there was a man inside with a gun!

THE INVASION IS CANCELLED

Would the Home Guard have been able to hold off a German invasion?

No chance!!

Well, maybe not, but we'll never know, because in September 1940 Hitler changed his mind and decided not to invade Britain after all.

Why?

Well, the RAF was proving a very difficult enemy to beat. And anyway, why would he waste men and tanks, when he could just as easily bomb British towns and cities directly from the air until the people begged him for mercy? Britain was about to be on the receiving end of a hideous barrage of horrors from the sky!

CHAPTER THREE
NITS
IN THE BLITZ

Hitler's plan was to bomb London and Britain's other big cities to bits. He thought this would cause so much suffering it would force the British to surrender. The German bombers began their onslaught in September 1940 . . .

They dropped more bombs in October 1940 . . .

Even more in November . . .

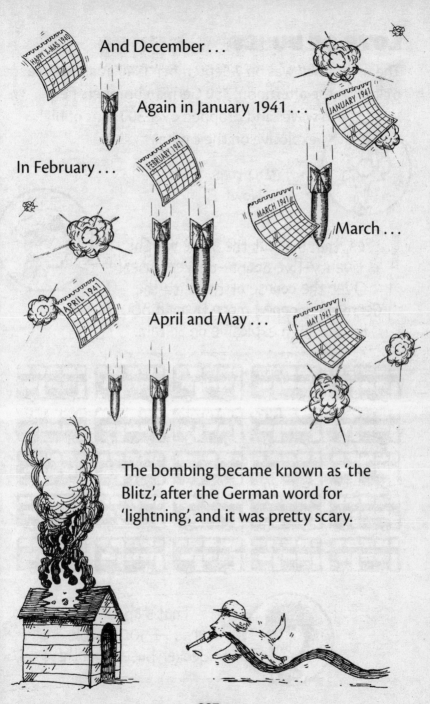

And December . . .

Again in January 1941 . . .

In February . . .

March . . .

April and May . . .

The bombing became known as 'the Blitz', after the German word for 'lightning', and it was pretty scary.

LOTS OF BUSES

The first attack was on 7 September 1940 at about five o'clock in the afternoon. 350 German bombers flew in waves and dropped over 300 tons of high explosive on the capital.

300 tons, Wow!

Yes, that's about the same weight as twenty-five double-decker buses! Over the course of the Blitz the Germans dropped more than 18,800 tons of high explosive on Britain.

That's about . . . er . . . 1,500 double-decker buses' worth!

For over ten hours the bombing went on and on. Explosions rocked the streets, buildings burned, and on the River Thames, boats blazed. As night fell, the sky glowed orange. 436 people were killed and 1,600 were seriously injured.

If you're wondering what you have to do to be 'seriously injured' . . .

. . . as opposed to mildly injured, or just putting it on for a bit of sympathy and a cup of tea . . .

. . . you've got to have fractured or broken something, be bleeding inside, be burned, crushed, smashed to bits or knocked unconscious. In other words, it's preferable to being killed . . . but only just.

The following morning the bombing finally stopped. Everyone came out of hiding to look at all the damage. There were giant holes in the ground where buildings had been, bits of arms and legs lying in the street, and smoke and dust everywhere . . .

It was horrible, but there wasn't much time to clean up – the bombers came back the next night . . . and the next. They bombed London for fifty-eight nights on the trot! While the Blitz went on, nobody got much sleep.

Central London was smashed to pieces during the Blitz, but St Paul's Cathedral was spared

But it wasn't just London that was on the receiving end of all these deadly explosions. Lots of other big British cities were hit. It was particularly dangerous for people who lived near railways, factories and ports, because the Germans considered them important targets and wanted to destroy them. In fact no one was totally safe, because if the planes couldn't find anything important to bomb, they just dropped their deadly load anywhere.

EATING TOOTHPASTE

The British government had realized that the Germans might try to bomb Britain's cities, so they'd stockpiled coffins and sandbags, handed out instruction leaflets and set up warning systems. They also wanted to try and make sure that Britain's kids were safe. Soon after the war began, a plan was launched to move 800,000 children out of the cities and into the countryside where they were less likely to be bombed. It was called 'Operation Pied Piper'!

'Operation Pied Piper'?

Yeah, remember that bloke in the flash tights with the flute, who got all the kids to follow him? That's what the government was doing. Geddit?

What, dressing up and playing a flute?

In towns everywhere, kids turned up at school and were given labels with a name, address and number on them. Once they'd put them on, they looked a bit like awkward-shaped parcels.

FAR FROM HOME

They were put on to buses and trains and shipped out (or 'evacuated') to towns and villages in the countryside. They were known as 'evacuees'.

They never knew exactly where they were going; they were just told to take enough food for two days. One girl evacuee got so hungry on the journey she ate her toothpaste!

When they finally arrived at their destination, they had to line up while local people came and took a look, chose which kid they wanted, and took them home.

Some kids loved it. They stayed with nice families, enjoyed the fresh air and made lots of new friends. But others had a horrible time. They missed their homes and were picked on by the locals for being smelly, dirty townies. Some evacuees came from poor city slums and had never seen a cow or eaten a vegetable in their entire life. Their host families complained that they were covered in lice, didn't know how to use a toilet and were scared of baths. One host mother asked if she could swap her evacuees for some different ones, because hers were 'rough and rude'.

London kids evacuated to Wales

Some hosts were too doddery to look after their evacuee children properly, while others were really nasty and beat them or locked them in cupboards. Perhaps it's not surprising that two-thirds of evacuee kids went back home within a few months!

SCHOOL'S OUT!

Whether you were in the countryside or the city, the good news was that you probably weren't in school.

As soon as war broke out, schools everywhere closed. Adults were too busy with war-stuff to worry about whether kids could add two plus four or spell the word 'giraffe'.

Within weeks there were complaints that children were running wild in the streets, so makeshift schools were set up in homes and churches, and open-air lessons were held in local parks.

Eventually most schools re-opened, although if there had been an air-raid the night before, school kids got the next morning off to catch up on their sleep!

An open-air school

SMELLING OF PEARDROPS

One of the things you practised at school (when it was open) was how to put on your gas mask.

The government gave out millions of weird-looking facemasks in case the Germans dropped bombs that gave off poisonous gas. Everyone had to carry one and had to learn how to put it on in a hurry.

HOW TO PUT ON A GAS MASK

1 Remove it from its box.

2 Put it on your face.

3 Breathe.

Sounds easy-peasy, but you'd be surprised how tricky this was, particularly if a bomb had just fallen through your roof and your house was on fire. So kids had to practise every day.

HOW TO DETECT POISON GAS

☐ Tear Gas smells like peardrops.

☐ Blister Gas smells like geraniums.

☐ Poison Gas smells of mown grass.

If you smell any of these things, it's time to get your mask on quick.

BLITZ QUIZ

What is the sensible thing to do when bombs start falling from the sky? Is it ...

1 Stand in the street, stare up at the sky, point and say 'Oooohhh, *see that really big bomb? It looks like it's coming this* ... *AAAARRRGHHH!!*'?

2 Run round in circles, scream and wet yourself?

3 Find a place to shelter, preferably somewhere under the ground with a very thick concrete ceiling?

If you didn't choose **3**, you'd better hope some loving family member comes round to scrape your smoking remains into a shoebox.

Lots of people built air-raid shelters in their gardens (which looked a bit like little metal sheds covered in earth).

Oi!

Others crowded into basements and cellars. Some went into the London Underground and slept on the platforms of the tube stations. This became so popular that there were queues outside the stations every evening. Eventually, the electricity was turned off at night, and from then on people could even sleep on the rails!

By the end of the Blitz more than 100,000 Londoners were sleeping in the Underground – so many that the government started providing them with bunk beds and toilets.

OUCH!

Enemy bomber pilots found their way around by looking at the ground below. At night from the air most countries are a network of tiny glittering lights – little bright ones where the roads are, and clusters of them twinkling away in the towns and cities.

To make it harder for the pilots to find their targets, the government ordered a 'black-out' at night. This meant that absolutely no light was allowed. Windows had to be covered with thick black fabric or black paint, streetlights were turned off and you had to pay a fine if you were caught striking a match or shining a torch.

It was a good idea, but there were a few problems. People drove into trees, walked into lamp posts or fell into rivers while trying to find their way round after dark. Burglars and pickpockets no longer had to worry about being seen, and the crime rate soared.

To try and make life safer, kerbs and tree trunks were painted white and people were encouraged to wear white clothes that showed up in the dark . . . nevertheless people still kept bumping into things.

The government eventually gave in and said people could carry torches – as long as they were covered in two sheets of tissue paper and were held downward!

STOP THE BOMBERS

Two kinds of weapon were invented to try and stop the bombers:

THE BARRAGE BALLOON: These were giant silver whale-sized helium balloons that floated in the sky, attached to the ground by steel cables. Any plane that got caught in the cables would get its wings ripped off. The German pilots had to fly really high to avoid them, which made their bombs less accurate.

THE ACK-ACK GUN (or Anti-aircraft Gun): These were designed to shoot German bombers out of the sky. They were ginormous, with 15-ft barrels (more than twice the height of a man). You needed a crew of eleven people to work each gun – two to wind the handles to position it, one to fire it, and eight to help load the massive shells.

Despite the guns and balloons, some bombers always got through, large parts of cities were destroyed, and more than 40,000 people were killed. Bombs also damaged famous landmarks like Buckingham Palace and Westminster Abbey.

THE SUICIDE SQUAD

Not all bombs exploded immediately. One of the worst jobs in the war was getting rid of the ones which hadn't gone off. The people who did this were called the 'Bomb Disposal Squad' (otherwise known as the 'Suicide Squad'). One bomb-disposal expert, Lieutenant Talbot, was awarded a medal for bravery because he picked up a live time-bomb and carried it on his shoulder 200 yards to a safe place before it exploded!

WELL DONE, BOY

They gave medals to animals as well. The first went to a dog called 'Chum', who helped dig his owner out of a collapsed air-raid shelter.

EAT YOUR HAT!

Despite all the bombs, destruction and death, most people tried to carry on as normal. They kept on working and going out at night (there was even a new dance called the 'black-out stroll'). Wrecked shops put out signs saying 'Business as Usual'.

One woman who was standing on the doorstep of her bombed-out house was asked how she felt. She said, 'Hitler can eat his hat for all I care. London folk will never give in.'

Neither will London dogs!

CHAPTER FOUR
FIGHT!
FIGHT! FIGHT!
FIGHT!

You may be thinking that the war was just between Germany and Britain. But if you are, you're wrong.

There was us!

And us!

And us!

Don't forget us!

What about us?

Germany and Britain both had 'Allies' – other countries all over the world who joined in to help them try and win.

NOT YOUR BEZZY MATES

People who join up with you in order to fight someone else are called your 'Allies'. They may not be your bezzy mates, but if you stick together, you've got a better chance of winning.

Suppose the school bully picked on you. You might want to form an 'alliance' with as many classmates as possible in the hope that they'd stand by you and stop you getting clobbered. Of course, they might run away at the crucial moment. But that's the problem with 'allies': they aren't real friends and sometimes they change sides.

When World War Two broke out, lots of countries became Allies with either Britain or Germany, although a few of them (like Russia) changed sides halfway through!

Germany's Allies included . . .

Italy,

Japan,

Ciao!

Sziasztok!

Hungary,

Romania and

Bulgaria.

Zdrave!

We call the people who fought with Britain 'The Allies', while the ones who fought on Germany's side called themselves 'The Axis Powers'.

An 'axis' is the name for anything which other things revolve round. Basically the Germans and their allies thought that the world revolved around them! They were real big-heads!

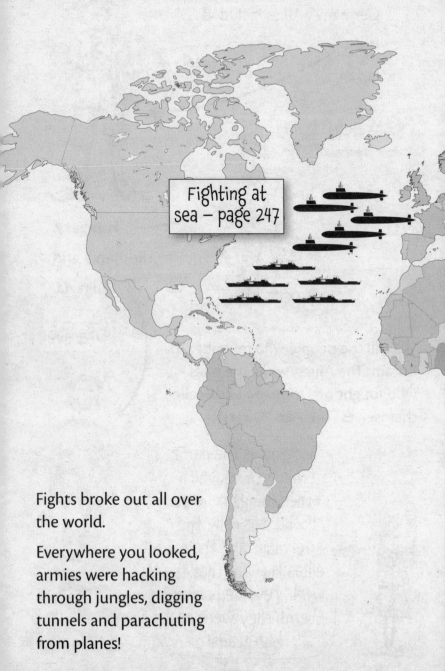

Fighting at
sea – page 247

Fights broke out all over
the world.

Everywhere you looked,
armies were hacking
through jungles, digging
tunnels and parachuting
from planes!

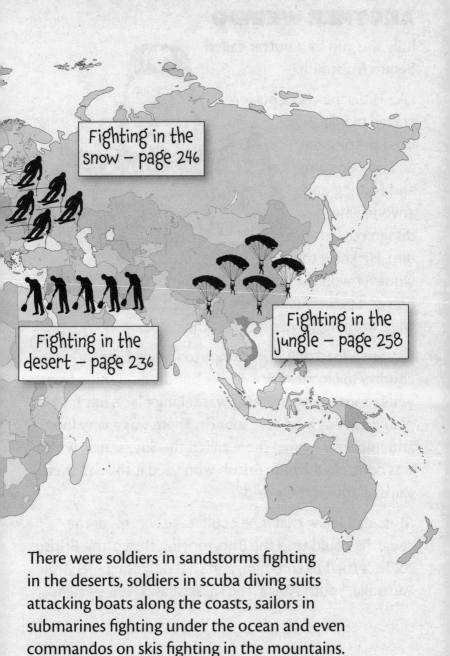

Fighting in the
snow – page 246

Fighting in the
desert – page 236

Fighting in the
jungle – page 258

There were soldiers in sandstorms fighting
in the deserts, soldiers in scuba diving suits
attacking boats along the coasts, sailors in
submarines fighting under the ocean and even
commandos on skis fighting in the mountains.

ANOTHER WEIRDO

Italy was run by a nutter called Benito Mussolini.

Like Hitler, he was a power-crazed maniac who liked putting on an army uniform and beating up anyone who disagreed with him. He knew that whoever won the war would become rich and powerful, so when it looked like the Germans were winning, he joined in on their side.

He sent a load of Italian troops to invade Egypt, a country in North Africa. It was hundreds of miles from where most of the fighting was taking place, but his plan wasn't as mad as it sounds. There was a very long and important canal there called the Suez Canal, which was controlled by the British who used it to send their ships all round the world.

Mussolini knew that if he could take control of the canal, he could stop the Brits moving their army. British soldiers tried to stop him, and so did fighting men from Australia, South Africa, the Far East and New Zealand.

In fact, millions of people from Africa, India and the Caribbean were sent halfway round the world to fight for the Brits during the war.

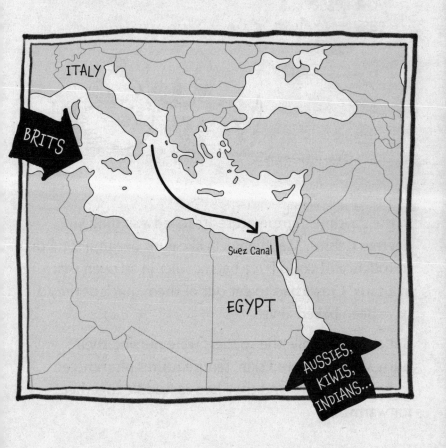

ITALY

BRITS

Suez Canal

EGYPT

AUSSIES, KIWIS, INDIANS...

SOLDIERS IN THE DESERT

Unfortunately, Egypt just happens to be surrounded by the Sahara desert, one of the hottest and driest places on earth, and fighting in a desert is hard work.

On the other hand, fighting in a dessert is easy – you just eat it!

In the daytime, temperatures reached a sizzling 50 degrees Celsius. Metal objects like guns became too hot to touch, and you'd have been cooler in an oven than in a tank. Crews had to get out of them quick or they'd have been baked alive!

But at night, while the soldiers were nursing their burned and blistered skin, temperatures plummeted to below freezing, and they had to huddle together for warmth.

237

And as for the sand, it got everywhere!

Sandstorms could last for days, and you couldn't see anything or anyone. Sometimes soldiers wandered off to the loo, got lost and were never seen again.

The Sahara desert is huge, and there were no towns or supplies for hundreds of miles, so armies had to carry their food and water with them over incredibly long distances. Soldiers sometimes even washed in petrol to save water . . . and all that was before the enemy started shooting at you!

VERY HARD BLOKES!

The Allies had a special force of soldiers whose job was to travel behind enemy lines in the desert and spy on what the Germans were doing. They were really tough and had to live in the Sahara for weeks with just poisonous snakes for company. They navigated by the stars and learned how to read tracks in the sand so they could tell how many men, tanks and camels had crossed in which direction.

In 1941, nine of them were left stranded in the desert without transport. All they had to survive on were three gallons of water, a packet of nine biscuits, a piece of chocolate and a compass that had been rescued from a burning vehicle. In order to make their escape they had to walk 200 miles. Their sandals fell to pieces, so they wrapped their feet in cloth torn from their jackets. After eight days braving the heat, the cold and the dust storms they finally made it to the nearest oasis!

THE DEVIL'S GARDEN

One of the big dangers in the desert was accidentally stepping on a landmine and getting your leg, hand, arm, head or all four blown off. Landmines were bombs hidden under the sand, which exploded when you stepped on them or drove over one in a tank.

Before the Battle of El Alamein in 1942 the Germans and Italians buried an incredible 500,000 mines across a five-mile strip of land to stop the Allies reaching them. They called this massive minefield the 'Devil's Garden'.

Allied engineers were sent to clear paths through the minefield and they didn't have lots of hi-tech kit to help them.

Both sides used mines. This is an Italian bomb-disposal team

HOW TO CLEAR A PATH THROUGH A MINEFIELD WITHOUT HI-TECH KIT

1 Walk along, using your bayonet to prod the ground until you hear the clink of metal.

Slowly!

Gently!

2 Clear the dirt and sand away.

Carefully!

3 Make sure the mine's not connected by wires to any other mines nearby, then gently lift it out.

Gently I said!

4 De-fuse it by unscrewing it and removing the detonator from inside, all without accidentally setting it off!

Aargh, it's too scary, I can't look!!

At El Alamein, the engineers had to do this hundreds of times while gunfire echoed all around them. Eventually they managed to clear paths through the minefield which allowed the Allies to attack. The victory at El Alamein helped the Allies to win the Desert War. The Italians and Germans left North Africa in May 1943.

PEEWEE'S GUIDE TO SOLDIERS' STUFF

Each army gave its soldiers slightly different bits and pieces to carry, but most of them were kitted out with . . .

A GAS MASK In case of a gas attack. They were heavy, were hardly ever needed and lots of soldiers left them behind or pretended they'd lost them.

RATIONS Soldiers in the field mostly lived on tinned beef, biscuits and the odd bit of chocolate. American soldiers were given packets of M&Ms.

A HOUSEWIFE No, not a tiny woman you put in your pocket. It was the soldiers' name for a sewing kit. It was for mending rips in your clothing and generally stopping all your clothes falling off.

A RIFLE This was a gun with a long barrel, so accurate it could hit an enemy up to 300m away.

A BAYONET If you missed, you could screw this handy dagger-like attachment on the end of your rifle, run up to your enemy and stab him!

SPARE SOCKS You'd sell your granny for a nice dry pair of these.

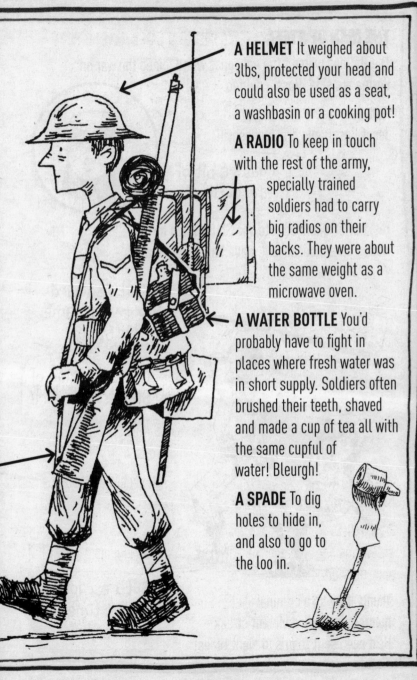

A HELMET It weighed about 3lbs, protected your head and could also be used as a seat, a washbasin or a cooking pot!

A RADIO To keep in touch with the rest of the army, specially trained soldiers had to carry big radios on their backs. They were about the same weight as a microwave oven.

A WATER BOTTLE You'd probably have to fight in places where fresh water was in short supply. Soldiers often brushed their teeth, shaved and made a cup of tea all with the same cupful of water! Bleurgh!

A SPADE To dig holes to hide in, and also to go to the loo in.

THE MAN OF STEEL

The Italians weren't the only ones who'd joined the war on Germany's side. Russia did too.

Its leader was a man called Josef Besarionis dze Jughashvili.

> That's a bit of a mouthful!

Yes, but he changed it to Joe Stalin when he was in prison because it made him sound hard.

> What's so hard about your name, Mr Stalin?

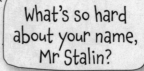

> It means 'Man of Steel', little girl!

Young Joe was a criminal mastermind with a violent streak. He'd been sent to prison eight times!

> But I escaped seven times, ho ho ho!

He'd been involved in street brawls, bank robberies, kidnapping, arson attacks and murder.

He wasn't just a dumb thug, though: he had big ambitions – he wanted to rule Russia. He joined a political party called the 'Bolsheviks' and used his criminal skills and stolen money to help get them into power. When the leader of the party died, Stalin took over. Once he was in charge, he ruled the country with an iron fist, imprisoning or murdering anyone he didn't like (one guy he **really** didn't like was found dead with an ice-pick in his head).

Whoops!

When the Second World War started, Stalin joined in on Germany's side. He wanted more land in Eastern Europe and thought now was a good time to grab it.

SOLDIERS ON SKIS

While some soldiers were fighting in the deserts of Africa, others were battling in deep snow . . . and it was all because of Stalin.

Soon after the war broke out, the Russian leader ordered hundreds of thousands of Russian soldiers and tanks to invade the neighbouring country of Finland.

The Finns were outnumbered and outgunned, but they had one big advantage – they were used to the weather. Finland lies on the edge of the Arctic circle – which means it gets cold . . . *really* cold . . . colder than a snowman in a freezer.

The Finns fought on skis and wore white padded uniforms, which kept them warm and made them invisible in the snowy landscape. They used to sneak up on the Russian troops, attack them and disappear back into the forest.

One Finnish soldier known as the 'White Death' terrified the Russians – he shot over 500 of them.

It wasn't just soldiers and airmen who fought in World War Two. All round the world, sailors were risking their lives too.

SOLDIERS UNDERWATER

Battles weren't only being fought on land. In the Atlantic Ocean another war was being waged between ships and submarines.

Britain and her Allies needed ships to transport food, guns and soldiers all over the globe.

But the Germans sent submarines called 'U-Boats' (short for Undersea Boats) to sink them. Groups of U-Boats would hunt in packs looking for ships to attack.

When they found one, they'd fire torpedoes into the ship's hull to try and sink it.

U-boats sank over 2,600 Allied ships during World War Two!

SWINE BOATS

Lots of U-Boat crews spent as long as six months at sea without stopping at one single port. During all that time they weren't allowed to bathe, shave or change their clothes.

The food on board a U-Boat got covered in mould — loaves of bread were nicknamed 'rabbits' because they were so white and furry!

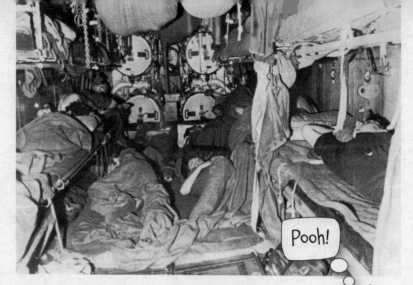

Pooh!

It was hot, damp and cramped, and with a crew of fifty men on board, the U-Boats soon got pretty stinky! In fact they were given the nickname 'swine boats' because of the smell! When they got to shore, all the bed clothes were burned – they were too filthy to be kept.

The British got fed up with German U-Boats attacking their ships all the time, so they made sure that they travelled in groups – called 'convoys' – protected by armed warships with plenty of firepower.

Ships also used listening devices to detect submarines underwater, so if there was a ship on the surface the entire U-Boat crew had to be totally silent, sometimes for hours at a time. They could only talk in whispers, and if they flushed the loo by mistake they'd probably be bombed to pieces!

CHAPTER FIVE
THE
YANKS
ARE COMING

By the summer of 1941, lots of countries had joined in on Hitler's side: he'd conquered most of Europe, blitzed Britain, and his U-Boats had sunk a load of ships.

My plan's going pretty well, don't you think?

It was time to put the next bit of it into action. Since the beginning of the war he'd been secretly plotting to conquer Russia, wipe out the people living there and replace them with Germans. So he now ordered his army to invade it, even though the Russians were on his side.

In June 1941 a gigantic force of nearly 4 million soldiers, 3,350 tanks, 60,000 motor vehicles and 625,000 horses moved into Russia. The Russians were taken completely by surprise. In the quickest advance in human history, the German army travelled nearly 200 miles into Russian territory in just one week.

So did that mean the end of the Russians? No, luckily for them, three things slowed the German advance:

1 **Its Size.** Russia was the largest country in the world, stretching halfway across the planet. It was absolutely, stonkingly, eye-wateringly ginormous. Even the Germans struggled to conquer it.

2 **The Weather.** First it rained and then it snowed. The wet weather turned the dirt roads into muddy bogs and then into frozen muddy bogs. The Germans weren't prepared for the cold – they stuffed newspaper in their jackets to try to warm themselves up, but it didn't do much good. They caught pneumonia, their fingers and toes dropped off from frostbite, and many soldiers froze to death.

3 **The Red Army.** The Russian Army was known as the 'Red Army' – it was massive (almost 2 million fighting men, thousands of tanks and tons of weapons) – and it fought like crazy to stop the Germans in their tracks. Mind you, it had to; Stalin made sure that if any of his men ran away, they were shot and their families were thrown in prison.

A German lorry stuck in the Russian mud, 1942

By the winter of 1941, the Germans were bogged down in the middle of Russia. This was bad news for Hitler and good news for Britain. Not only had Russia changed sides, but most of the German army were now freezing their bums off in Russia, rather than attacking the Brits.

OK, so Stalin was a psychopathic lunatic but at least now he was OUR psychopathic lunatic.

Meanwhile there was a second bit of good news for the Allies. Guess who else was about to join in on their side?

JAPAN MAKES A BIG MISTAKE

Halfway across the world, Japan became Germany's ally. Like Hitler and Stalin, the Japanese wanted an Empire. They decided to take over all the thousands of islands in the Pacific Ocean. Their plan was that the Germans would rule the West, while they would have their own island-empire in the East.

In December 1941, they sent in troops to seize some of the bigger Pacific islands. They knew that if they acted quickly, the Allies would be caught by surprise and wouldn't be able to stop them.

At the same time they sent planes and submarines to destroy a fleet of American ships in Pearl Harbor on the island of Hawaii. They thought everyone would be so

shocked and impressed at the speed of their invasion and the suddenness of their attacks, that they'd back off and let Japan keep its new territory.

They were wrong. These tactics just made everyone really, *really* angry; and the angriest of all were the Americans.

Boy! We're really, really mad!

Until then they'd stayed out of the war.

They'd helped the Allies a bit by giving them money, weapons and aircraft, but they didn't want to send over actual soldiers in case they got shot. But *now* Japan had attacked American ships. As one Japanese general said, 'I fear we have awakened a sleeping tiger . . .'

THE MAN IN A WHEELCHAIR

Franklin Delano Roosevelt caught a horrible virus called polio, and had to spend the rest of his life in a wheelchair. But did that stop him? . . . Did it heck!

No, not only did he become the President of the United States, but he turned out to be one of the best Presidents the Americans had ever had.

When Japan attacked those ships at Pearl Harbor, Roosevelt decided it was time for America to go to war, bigtime!

Roosevelt was hardly ever photographed in his wheelchair. A lot of Americans didn't even know he used one

SURPRISE, SURPRISE!

The Japanese surprised everybody ... and nobody was more surprised than the British.

They couldn't have been more surprised if the Japanese had jumped out of a giant cake wearing a gorilla costume and holding a big banner saying 'SURPRISE!'

Surprise Number 1: Britain had a big colony in South East Asia called 'British Malaya'. It included a giant military base on the island of Singapore which the British thought the Japanese would never dare attack.

But they were wrong. On 8 December 1941 the Japanese invaded that too.

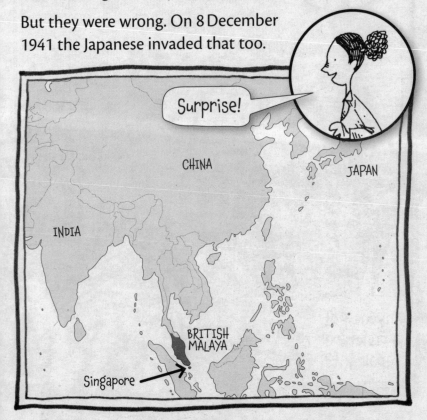

Surprise!

CHINA

JAPAN

INDIA

BRITISH MALAYA

Singapore

Surprise Number 2: Even if the Japanese did attack, the British had been confident they would attack by sea. So they'd built lots of walls, forts and guns around Singapore pointing out towards the water.

But the Japanese didn't attack from the sea: they came through the jungles and swamps to the north. Lots of them used bicycles and cycled along the jungle paths.

Surprise!

Anyone got a puncture repair kit?

Surprise Number 3: The British also had loads of planes and ships that could be used to scare off attackers.

But at the same time as bombing Pearl Harbor, the Japanese also bombed the British airbases on Singapore, so all their planes were destroyed. And when the British sent ships to stop the Japanese, they were sunk by torpedoes.

Surprise!

Surprise Number 4: Even if it did come to an actual battle, the British had a massive army, which would soon stop the Japanese in their tracks. Everybody knew the Japanese were rubbish at fighting and would give in easily.

But the Japanese turned out to be battle-hardened and bloodthirsty fighters who attacked with speed and ferocity. The British army was soon retreating and by February 1942 the Japanese had taken Singapore, and over 60,000 British, Indian and Australian soldiers were killed or captured.

Surprise!

British soldiers in Singapore surrender to the Japanese

Churchill called the fall of Singapore the worst disaster in British military history.

It was going to take the help of the Americans to stop the Japanese advance. By March 1942, American ships and troops were flooding into the Pacific.

GOING MAD IN THE JUNGLE

Thousands of American soldiers were sent to recapture the Pacific islands. The weather was hot and humid and the islands were often covered in thick jungle and swamps. In the rainy season, everything got soaked and the soldiers' uniforms and kit rotted. Wounds didn't heal and they got pus-filled ulcers on their skin which attracted flies. Crocodiles lurked in the rivers and ate the dead bodies after each battle. Clouds of mosquitoes spread malaria which caused fevers, vomiting and hallucinations.

To make matters worse, the Japanese soldiers were as scary as scary can be!

GUTS ON THE GROUND

For centuries the people of Japan had been isolated from the rest of the world, ruled over by of warriors known as the 'Samurai'.

You didn't want to annoy the Samurai. They were the only people who were allowed to own swords and fight anyone who didn't show them enough respect. They lived by a strict code known as the 'Way of the Warrior'. If a Samurai was ever defeated in battle, he had to kill himself by using his own sword to cut his stomach open so his guts would fall out!

By the time World War Two began, the Samurai didn't rule Japan any more, but lots of Japanese soldiers still believed in the Samurai code of fighting to the death and killing themselves rather than surrendering.

IWO JIMA

The Americans attacked each island in the Pacific one-by-one and recaptured them – a slow and agonizing process.

One of the last islands they took back was called Iwo Jima. It was defended by 22,000 Japanese soldiers who had built pillboxes all over it connected by a network of deep trenches, tunnels and 'spider holes' (holes in the ground with just enough room for one person to jump out and shoot you).

THE LEAST FUN PLACE TO BE IN WORLD WAR TWO

The Japanese thought any soldier who surrendered (without first gutting themselves in shame) deserved no respect. Japanese officers often treated captured soldiers like a piece of particularly smelly dog poo on the bottom of their shoe. Many troops from the British Empire were treated with vile cruelty, but Americans had a terrible time too.

One American soldier, Albert Parker, remembered being captured by the Japanese at a place called Bataan in 1942. He was made to march to a prison camp 65 miles away along, with thousands of other Prisoners of War. They didn't have any food and had to drink dirty ditch water to stay alive; any stragglers were beaten to death or bayoneted; the fallen were decapitated by Japanese officers swinging samurai swords.

In 1945, 60,000 US soldiers landed on the island, backed up by 800 warships. The Japanese were forced back, but fought every step of the way, shooting, stabbing with bayonets and hurling themselves at the attackers. One hill in particular was nicknamed the 'meat grinder' because so many soldiers died when the Americans tried to capture it. Even after the Japanese knew they'd lost control of the island, they charged towards the enemy screaming and trying to wipe out more enemy soldiers before getting shot themselves.

Iwo Jima cost the Americans the lives of almost 6,000 soldiers, with another 17,000 wounded – all to capture an island only five miles long.

This statue in Washington DC commemorates the raising of the American flag on Iwo Jima

KAMIKAZE!

It wasn't just Japanese soldiers who resorted to crazy tactics. Japanese pilots volunteered to carry out suicide missions, flying their planes straight into Allied ships and blowing them up. These flights were known as 'Kamikaze missions' (Kamikaze means 'divine wind').

Tactics like this might sound mad but they scared the bejeebies out of the American troops. They thought the Japanese were barking mad – and no one likes fighting mad people: they might do anything!

MEANWHILE IN ITALY . . .

Rome is here

American troops didn't
just fight in the Pacific.
Three days after declaring war on
Japan, the USA declared war on
Germany and Italy as well.

Now the Americans were on their side,
the Allies decided to launch a fresh attack.
In 1943 Allied
forces invaded
southern Italy using
soldiers from Britain,
America, Canada, India,
New Zealand and Poland.

Allies land here

They thought this would be a doddle, and
reckoned they'd be sitting in a nice restaurant in
Rome within weeks, eating spaghetti bolognese with
a sprinkle of parmesan cheese. At first, it looked like
they'd be right. The Italians knew they didn't stand a
chance and soon surrendered. But that wasn't the end
of the story – not by a long shot!

Monte Cassino looked pretty before the war . . .

The Italians might have given up but the Germans had other ideas. They moved into Italy and fought to stop the Allies getting any further.

Nevertheless the Allied troops slowly pushed north through Italy, but it was tough going – the only route to [...] as through the mountains! It was wet and cold, [...] was rocky and the only shelter was a few [...]hes, with booby traps, barbed wire, and [...]nderneath!

Monte Cassino was a famously beautiful monastery in the mountains – or at least it *was*, until it became the focus of a long and bloody battle. It was bombed time and time again and attacked by waves of soldiers as they tried to dislodge the Germans from the site. It took six months and four big battles to take over the monastery. By the end, all that remained was a smoking heap of rubble!

The Allied troops finally reached Rome in June 1944.

CHAPTER SIX
HOW TO BECOME A SPY

Pssst!
Reader!

Who, me?

Yes. Can you keep a secret?

Sure.

Even a really juicy one?

Yes.

Can you lie convincingly under pressure?

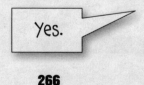
Yes.

Even when someone's giving you a Chinese burn or your mum's staring at you with a cross face?

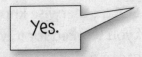

Yes.

Can you be really really sneaky, like taking the last Chocolate Hobnob and pretending the dog ate it?

Yes.

Then congratulations, you'll make an excellent spy. You'd better start practising foreign languages and building up a collection of fake moustaches right away, so you'll be ready when you get tapped on the shoulder and are asked to become a member of . . .

CHURCHILL'S SECRET ARMY!!

SHHHHH!!

Winston Churchill realized that it was going to take more than luck to win the war, so he set up a secret organization called the 'Special Operations Executive' (or SOE), otherwise known as Churchill's Secret Army. If you worked for it, you became a spy and your job was to travel secretly into Nazi-controlled Europe. You had to pass on any useful information, and blow up enemy trains, factories and bridges. At the height of the war there were over 13,000 people doing this very dangerous job – anyone caught was arrested, horribly tortured and then shot by a firing squad.

SPY SCHOOL

If you were brave and clever enough to join the secret squad, you were taught useful things like map-reading, unarmed combat and how to use dangerous weapons. But you also learned a whole host of other sneaky tricks, like how to pick locks, copy keys, write secret messages and blow things up before walking away whistling and pretending you didn't have anything to do with it.

Then you were parachuted into enemy territory, and in order to avoid being detected, you learned how to jump out of a plane at a low height without squishing into the ground.

You also had to wear a disguise, and were given a fake name and a 'cover story'. This meant making up things like where you were born, who your mum and dad were, and how many brothers and sisters you had, so that if anyone asked, your lies would be really convincing.

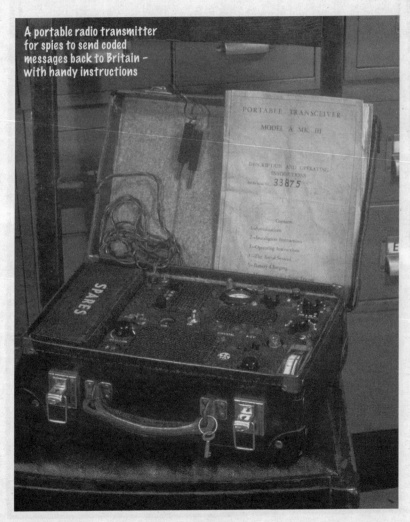

A portable radio transmitter for spies to send coded messages back to Britain – with handy instructions

BEAUTIFUL AND DANGEROUS

Lots of Churchill's spies were women. They were chosen because they'd arouse less suspicion. Who would suspect Mrs Brown round the corner, in her woolly cardigan and baggy tights, of being an undercover spy?

But some women were chosen because they were beautiful and deadly. Kyrstyna Skarbek was a Polish aristocrat. On one occasion she parachuted into France, chatted up some German guards, and persuaded them to release a group of British spies they'd captured. Another time she secretly skied over mountains and through blizzards to get into Poland and recruit Polish agents.

She narrowly escaped capture by the Nazis several times. Once she pretended to be seriously ill by biting her tongue so hard that she coughed up blood. Another time she was stopped by two German guards at a border crossing and produced two live grenades. When the guards ran away she chucked the grenades at them and escaped across the border!

CHURCHILL'S SPY TOY SHOP

Secret agents need secret weapons. In the Second
World War many were developed and stored in a secret
room in the Natural History Museum in London which
became known as 'Churchill's Toy Shop'.

Wow!

They even stuffed dead rats with explosives. They hoped that the enemy would want to get rid of the furry little bodies, and would throw them in the fire, which would then explode.

If you think all this sounds like something out of James Bond, you're not far wrong. The author Ian Fleming, who wrote the James Bond books, worked with the Special Operations Executive, and based his characters on real secret agents!

Churchill's Toy Shop

NEW FOR 1943!

false trail shoes

Sneaky!

FITS IN A SUITCASE!

MINI, FOLDING MOTORBIKE

BOMB
WITH ADDED POISON DARTS

BOMBS in disguise

fruit   poo*

Coal   Wood

Petrol Can.

*Choice of camel or horse poo

INVISIBLE INK

Shoe Knife
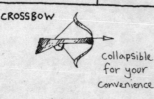
KIK

exploding Suitcase

CROSSBOW

Collapsible for your convenience

PIPE GUN
SUBTLE!

KA-BOOM!

Exploding Pen!

273

SECRET KIDS

The SOE weren't the only secret fighters. In every occupied country local people, like farmers, railway workers and housewives, fought the Nazis. They were known as 'The Resistance' because they resisted the enemy taking over their countries.

Sometimes Resistance fighters set up their own little armies in the mountains, but often, especially in the towns, they were as secret as Churchill's Secret Army, and sabotaged roads, railways and factories. Kids, who were unlikely to attract attention from the Germans, often became involved, running messages and helping Allied airmen get back to Britain.

A member of the French Resistance sets a bomb

THE SPY IN A COFFIN

One member of the French Resistance was a middle-aged woman called Berthe Fraser. To her neighbours she was just a normal housewife, but in secret she helped British agents working in France. She gave them shelter, arranged transport and safe hiding places, organized meetings and carried messages hidden in her bags of shopping. Once she was asked to help an important British spy travel across France without being detected, so she organized a funeral procession and hid him in the coffin!

Eventually the Germans captured her, put her in prison and tortured her. She was stripped and flogged in public but she refused to give away the names of her friends in the Resistance. She was rescued in September 1944 when the Allies stormed the camp where she was held. She is supposed to have said to her rescuers, 'Thank you, boys, you're just in time.'

BRAVE KIDS

Did you know that one of the first acts of resistance in the Second World War was carried out by a group of schoolkids? In November 1940, after the Nazis had taken over France, some French schoolchildren gathered in the centre of Paris and publicly celebrated the defeat of the Germans in World War One! This was a really dangerous thing to do. It was like sticking out your tongue at Hitler and blowing a raspberry at him – you can imagine how mad he could get if he thought people were taking the mickey out of him.

ESCAPE ARTISTS

When Allied fighters were captured, they became Prisoners of War and were put into big camps watched over by German guards. Many tried to escape and with the help of the Resistance some were successful.

One Prisoner-of-War camp in Poland called Stalag Luft III was the scene of some very daring escapes. For instance, a group of prisoners pretended to be doing exercises in the prison yard, taking turns jumping over a large box-like wooden vaulting horse. What the German guards didn't know was that underneath the horse, two prisoners were busy digging a tunnel!

At the end of each day they'd cover the tunnel entrance with a piece of wood, and shovel earth on top of it, then they'd be carried back to their huts inside the horse. After lots of vaulting, the tunnel was finally ready and three men managed to escape and return to Britain!

BRAINBOXES

One problem with trying to work out what the Germans were up to was that they sent all their messages in a complicated secret code. They'd invented a special machine, a bit like a typewriter, and when they typed a message in, the machine scrambled it all up.

It was called the 'Enigma Machine' – an 'enigma' is another word for a puzzle. The person you sent the message to had to have another machine and know the settings you used, so they could unscramble the message.

All the messages Britain and her Allies intercepted were total gobbledygook. This was incredibly frustrating. Imagine having a message in front of you that you KNOW is important but you can't read it! Grrrr . . .

So the British recruited lots of very clever mathematicians, engineers and scientists and told them to find out how the Enigma machine worked.

These brainboxes managed to get their hands on part of one of the German Enigma machines, then built an enormous computer the size of a room, which could calculate all the different settings and decipher the words. Now they could read all the enemy's messages and find out what they were planning – it was a massive advantage for the Allies!

See, it wasn't just the blokes fighting who won the war. Geeky people like me helped too!

CHAPTER SEVEN
CARROTS, CARROTS AND MORE CARROTS

Yum!

While British troops were fighting overseas, back home people was doing their bit for the war too.

I'm an ambulance driver!

Before it started, most women didn't have paid jobs. They left school, got married and spent their lives looking after their families, cleaning the house, cooking the tea, doing the washing and making sure everyone had clean pants for the next day. But when war broke out and most men were sent away to do the fighting, women were left to do all the other jobs that needed doing. In fact, without them the war effort would have ground to a halt.

281

They worked in factories, built planes, made guns, bombs and bullets, operated searchlights, fired anti-aircraft guns, drove fire engines, fixed cars, served as nurses in hospitals and worked in the fields growing and picking all the crops.

Then they went home, cooked the tea, cleaned the house, did the washing and made sure everyone had a clean pair of pants for the next day, just like before!!!

WOMEN AT WAR

Some women even joined the armed forces.

This is a picture of my mum, Phyllis Robinson, who was a corporal in the Women's Royal Air Force, and my dad, Leslie Robinson, who was in the RAF.

WHAT'S IN YOUR KNICKERS?

Before the war, Britain got most of its food from abroad. But as soon as the fighting started, German U-Boats began sinking the ships which brought supplies to the UK. Meanwhile some countries that had previously been our suppliers were now

Britain's enemies – so our food started running out.

Oi! Stop running out!

To make sure there was enough to go round, lots of foodstuffs were 'rationed', which meant you were only allowed a certain amount of them. Everyone got issued with a 'ration book' with coupons which told you how much you could have.

Even restaurants and hotels had to ration their food.
For instance, hotels were only allowed to serve
one-sixth of an ounce of butter with each meal . . .

That's a tiny sliver
about the thickness
of a pound coin!

There's enough butter here for
18,745 people . . . probably

This graffiti man appeared whenever something was in short supply. He's called Chad!

WOT! NO BANANAS?

Foods like lemons and bananas, which only grew in faraway countries, disappeared from the shops. And with the usual types of meat in short supply, people started eating rabbit, horse and even whale!

To cope with all these food shortages, families were encouraged to grow their own vegetables and keep tasty animals like hens, rabbits, goats and pigs in their back yards. Parks, gardens and even school playing fields were turned into giant vegetable patches! Some people bought food illegally, or even stole it. One woman who worked as a waitress smuggled pieces of salmon, steaks and kippers out of her restaurant in her knickers!

Fancy a nice chop?

WOT! NO CARROT CAKE?

One of the few things that wasn't in short supply was carrots, so everyone ended up eating lots of them. The government even designed a character called Dr Carrot who encouraged people to try carrot curry, carrot jam, toffee carrots and a drink called 'Carrolade' made out of, you guessed it, carrots.

DOCTOR CARROT
guards
your Health

But it wasn't just food that was in short supply. Petrol, clothing, coal, gas and electricity were rationed too, along with paper, furniture and soap. Even the number of pockets, buttons and pleats on your new clothes and the amount of lace you could put on a pair of frilly panties were restricted. Stockings were so hard to get hold of that women pretended they were wearing them, even though they weren't. They rubbed gravy browning on their legs, and drew the seams on with a pen!

SEARCH FOR SCRAP

So much metal was needed to make weapons that thousands of people sacrificed their aluminium cooking pots so they could be melted down and turned into metal for aircraft. One eighty-year-old granny walked a whole mile to hand in her old saucepan. But it wasn't just pots and pans that were sacrificed. People gave aluminium cigarette cases, bedsteads, bicycles, railings . . . someone even donated an artificial leg, and someone else a racing car! In one town so much was collected, they had to use a steam-roller to flatten it all before it was carried away.

Some people say that all this collecting was a big publicity stunt, and that lots of the scrap was never melted down. Instead it was just dumped in the River Thames.

But mysteriously all the government records about the scrap collection were destroyed — so we'll never know for sure!

Berlin in 1945

SHEER HELL

Things may have been difficult in Great Britain, but the people of some countries suffered much more.

For instance, in Russia, where the German and Russian armies were fighting for control of the city of Leningrad, life was sheer hell. The streets were a battleground and the Germans blocked off all supplies to the city and bombed the Russian food stores.

Food became so scarce that your entire daily food ration was 125 grams of bread (about four slices) which was mostly made up of sawdust! People ate anything they could, including their pets. More than half a million people died of hunger.

EVEN WORSE THAN SHEER HELL

The next three pages tell a very horrible story . . .

But it's also a very important one.

You decide whether you want to read it or not.

For Jewish people living in German-occupied countries, things got even worse. The Nazis rounded them up and forced them into 'ghettos', which were special areas of towns and cities where they were separated from the rest of the population. They were packed so tight that six people lived in each room!

Jewish familes forced out of their homes in Poland

When rations were introduced, Jewish people got less than anyone else and weren't allowed any meat, eggs, bread or milk. The Nazis knew this meant lots of them would starve, but when they didn't die quickly enough, Hitler's men decided on something even more drastic. They packed all the Jewish people they could find into trains and sent them to special camps.

Discarded Jewish clothing in a concentration camp

Once there, the fit and healthy ones were used as slave labour until they died of exhaustion. The old and the very young, including babies, children and the sick, were considered to be useless. They were herded into special chambers and poison gas was pumped in to kill them.

Some people risked their lives by hiding Jewish people in their houses, or helping them escape to other countries. German businessman Oskar Schindler protected the hundreds of Jewish people who worked in his factory in Poland. He persuaded the Nazis that they were doing valuable work for the war effort and couldn't be sent to the camps, and when it became too dangerous for them to stay at home he let them live in his factory. He is thought to have saved the lives of over 1,000 people.

Millions of Jews were murdered by the Nazis.

We must all try to make sure nothing like this ever happens again.

That's why saying 'NO' to racism is so important . . .

. . . whether it's at school, or on the playing field or among your friends.

Dogs wouldn't do anything like that. Humans can be really horrible sometimes.

CHAPTER EIGHT

D-DAY!

By spring 1944 the Red Army was beating the Germans in the snowy wastes of Russia, the Americans had joined in on the Allied side, and Mussolini's Italian army had been defeated. It was time to take Europe back from Hitler.

So the Allies planned a massive invasion – a huge army of British, American and Canadians who would cross the Channel and land in Normandy on the coast of France.

HOW TO FAKE AN INVASION

But they needed to build so many ships, planes and guns, that any German plane flying overhead would spot them and guess what was happening right away. How could they keep the invasion a surprise?

Their solution was to hatch the all-time sneakiest plan ever. They pretended the invasion was going to land somewhere else! That way Hitler would order his troops to defend the wrong place!

To fool him they created a pretend invasion force complete with inflatable rubber tanks and planes, dummy airfields and fake landing craft, and used sound systems on the back of trucks to broadcast the noise of an army on the move. They even broadcast fake radio messages between non-existent ships, while at the same time dropping bundles of tiny metallic strips from aircraft that gave the impression on enemy radar screens of a massive incoming bomber raid far inland. The Germans were totally fooled.

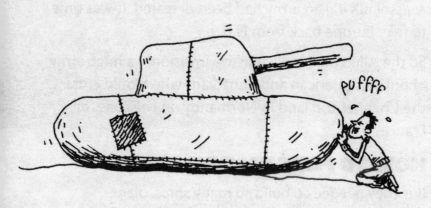

pufffff

In fact, the trick worked so well that when the real invading army landed, Hitler thought it was a diversion from the actual invasion and held off sending his army to stop it.

So now it was time for 'D-Day', the code-name for the day the real Allied invasion of Europe was planned to begin. If it worked, it was pretty certain that the Germans would be defeated. But first the Allied Army had to get ashore!

Just after midnight on 6 June 1944, 24,000 paratroopers were dropped into enemy territory. Their job was to block roads and capture bridges to stop the Germans sending in their army when they found out about the invasion.

But in the darkness and heavy fog, not all the paratroopers landed where they were supposed to. Some dropped into swamps, others splashed into ponds or ended up on the roofs of buildings. One paratrooper was left dangling from a church spire! (Whoops!) Others landed with their parachutes riddled with holes after being shot at by German guns. (Gulp!)

Nevertheless many of them managed to find their targets, and blew up bridges, cut phone lines and ambushed the German positions.

Then at 6.30 the next morning, the main invasion began. A massive force of over 150,000 troops landed on the beaches of Normandy.

And it wasn't just soldiers who came ashore. Boats delivered masses of food, guns, tanks, lorries and ammunition so that the invading army would have enough supplies.

This was the largest sea-borne invasion in history!

A DAY AT THE BEACH

The beach landings were no picnic. There was fierce fighting. Ships were fired at and exploded in huge balls of flame, men were shot or drowned as they tried to reach the beach.

Once on dry land, some soldiers were given orders to get to the top of 100-foot-high cliffs to try and destroy the German guns that were pointed at the beach. If they failed, so might the invasion. They fired rocket-propelled hooks up to the top of the cliffs, leaving ropes dangling down. As they made their wet and slippery way up the rock face, the Germans above shot at them and tried to cut their ropes! Eventually they made it to the top, and managed to find the German guns and destroy them before they could be used against the Allies below.

2,500 soldiers died on D-Day, but more than 150,000 made it safely to shore! The invasion had begun!

The D-Day invasion begins

The Allies begin to move into France

MAGIC BULLETS

The Allied soldiers carried 'magic bullets' with them. No, I don't mean they'd been conjured up by wizards with white beards who cast spells and made bullets magically hit their targets. That would have been ridiculous . . . although also very cool.

'Magic bullet' was the name doctors used for a special type of medicine – one that was so effective, it seemed to work by magic.

The soldiers had actually been given little packets of a special new drug called 'penicillin'. Before it was invented, lots of people died from small infections, because when they cut their skin, dirt got into it, along with lots of tiny living things called 'bacteria' which can spread infection.

Penicillin works by killing these bacteria, and during World War Two, scientists in Britain and America worked hard to produce stockpiles of the stuff. Finally, by D-Day there was enough to treat all the injured Allied soldiers involved in the invasion, which saved thousands of lives!

They never had that sort of thing in my day!

THE RACE FOR BERLIN

From the coast, the Allies then pushed inland. Meanwhile on the other side of Europe, Stalin's Red Army was pushing eastward. Hitler and the German army were trapped in the middle!

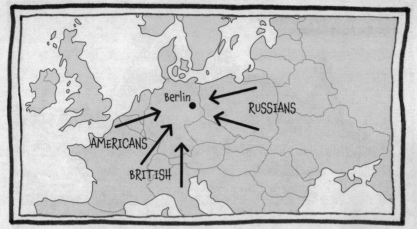

The British, American and Russian armies raced towards Germany's capital city, Berlin. At the same time, Allied planes dropped thousands of bombs on German cities to force them to surrender. In fact the Allies dropped more bombs on Berlin than the Germans dropped on the whole of Britain.

One German city called Dresden was so badly bombed that the whole city was flattened and the explosions caused a storm of fire which killed 25,000 German men, women and children.

GOODBYE, HITLER

In Berlin, Hitler ordered his men to defend the city to the death, while he hid in an underground bunker. But there weren't enough soldiers available, so kids from the Hitler Youth were given guns and helmets and told to fight the approaching Allied armies! Children as young as eight had to face some of the most battle-hardened soldiers in the world. Their chances of surviving were very low.

The German government building after the Allied bombing

Some people thought the Allied bombing was fair because it gave the Germans a taste of their own medicine.

Others reckoned it made the Allies just as bad as the Nazis.

What do you think?

302

Soon the Russian Red Army had reached the outskirts of Berlin. Meanwhile, down in his bunker, Hitler received news that in Italy his fellow dictator, Benito Mussolini, had been caught trying to run away, had been shot by a firing squad, and that an angry crowd had hung his body upside down from a meat hook.

Hitler finally realized the war was lost. Within days the Russians would be knocking on the door of his bunker, saying something like . . .

Hello, Mr Hitler, it's meat-hook time!

So two days later he poisoned his beloved pet dog Blondie and then shot himself. Germany surrendered. The war in Europe was over! Big celebrations broke out all over the world from Moscow to New York!

Celebrating in Trafalgar Square

Hooray! Back to the ironing and washing-up!

M 2 1256

There was only one *small* snag. Over in the Pacific, the war was still raging. The Japanese weren't going to give in easily!

THE WORLD'S DEADLIEST WEAPON

After six years and a lot of bloodshed most people were pretty sick of the war, so the Allies made a decision to end it quickly, the only way they knew how.

They would launch a weapon so deadly, so destructive and so mind-numbingly, jaw-droppingly terrifying, that the Japanese would give up immediately!

And the Americans had got exactly that kind of weapon. It was called 'the Atomic bomb' and it was 2,000 times more powerful than a normal bomb. The scientists knew that when it exploded, it would create a massive fireball, and would send out shockwaves which would flatten buildings for miles around. Just one bomb would wipe out a city. But the Allies decided to drop not one, but two!

One was bad enough, two was horrendous. But the Allies didn't want the Japanese to think they only had one of these new bombs — they wanted them to think they had loads!

HITLER'S BIG MISTAKE

Hitler's attack on the Jews wasn't just mean and stupid: it helped the Allies win the war.

When Hitler and the Nazis started picking on Jewish people, lots of clever Jewish scientists left Germany and went to live in Britain and America where they helped the Allies develop things like penicillin and the Atomic bomb!

THE NOT SO LITTLE 'LITTLE BOY'

The first bomb was code-named 'Little Boy'. Which was a pretty strange name considering it was over 3 metres long and weighed more than a minibus!

It was dropped by plane over the Japanese city of Hiroshima on 6 August 1945. When it hit the ground, there was a blinding light, followed by a giant,

boiling-black, mushroom-shaped cloud that rose over 33,000 feet into the sky. 70,000 people were killed instantly. Some were crushed by falling buildings or suffocated in the smoke. Others were burned to a crisp, or were simply vaporized.

But the bomb didn't just kill people, it also made them sick. It produced invisible rays and particles that damaged people's bodies, and gave them what was called 'radiation sickness'.

For instance, two days after the explosion, a fourteen-year-old boy who was feeling poorly was admitted to hospital. Then his hair began falling out and his nose started bleeding. Within three weeks he was dead. There was nothing the doctors could do! Other people who survived the blast got cancer or had children who were born with disabilities.

All this may have been terrible, but it wasn't the end. The second bomb was dropped on a city called Nagasaki three days later. The Japanese surrendered within a week.

The war was over, but ordinary Japanese people paid a huge price.

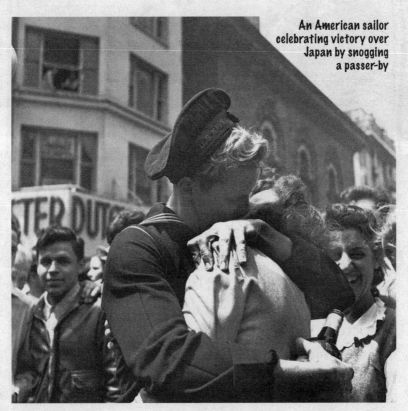

An American sailor celebrating victory over Japan by snogging a passer-by

DIDN'T ANYONE TELL YOU?

Actually, the war wasn't over for everyone.

Some Japanese soldiers fighting on remote islands in the Pacific never got the message! One soldier held out in the mountains of the Philippines for another 28 years. He hid in the jungle and shot at anyone who came near him, thinking they were the enemy. Several times people tried to tell him that the war had finished but he didn't believe them. In the end his old commander was found and was sent to the mountains to tell him that it really was all over!

WHAT HAPPENED NEXT?

After the war ended, the surviving soldiers went back to their homes and families, cities were rebuilt and most people got on with their lives again.

But lots of top German and Japanese officials were arrested and were put on trial by the Allies. Many were convicted of terrible cruelty and of starting a war that had cost millions of lives, and were sentenced to death by hanging.

UNITED NATIONS - NOT!

In 1945 the governments of the world got together and formed the 'United Nations'. This was a global peace-keeping force which tried to prevent massive wars from breaking out ever again.

But the peace only lasted about five minutes . . .

. . . and then countries started fighting each other like before, and wars have been happening ever since.

Luckily, none of them has been as big as the Second World War . . .

. . . and none of them has involved dropping another Atomic bomb.

Not yet anyway – paws crossed!

TIMELINE

1914–1918	The Great War, later known as the First World War
1929	The Great Depression begins, and is about as much fun as it sounds
1933	Hitler takes charge in Germany
1938	German troops march into Austria
May 1939	Germany and Italy become allies
1 Sep 1939	Germany invades Poland – surprise!
3 Sep 1939	Britain and France declare war on Germany
Nov 1939	Russia invades Finland for some very chilly fighting
May 1940	Winston Churchill becomes Prime Minister of Britain
28 May–4 Jun 1940	Dunkirk – 338,000 British soldiers are saved from the beach
Jun 1940	The Germans take over Paris
Jun 1940	Italy joins the war
Jul–Oct 1940	The Battle of Britain is fought in the air
7 Sep 1940	The Blitz – the German campaign of air raids on Britain – begins
Dec 1940	British soldiers start fighting the Italians in North Africa
Jun 1941	Germany invades Russia – surprise again!
Sep 1941–Jan 1944	Life in Leningrad gets much more horrendous during the very long German siege of the city

7 Dec 1941	Japan destroys American ships at Pearl Harbor in Hawaii. The Americans get so angry that they join in the war
15 Feb 1942	Singapore falls to the Japanese. The British are miffed
Oct–Nov 1942	Battle of El Alamein – actually the second Battle of El Alamein, but this one's a very important win for the Allies
Feb 1943	The Germans surrender at Stalingrad in Russia – a major loss
Feb 1943	Britain and America begin regular bombing of Germany
Jul 1943	Allied soldiers land in Sicily, getting ready to invade mainland Italy. Shortly afterwards, the Italians overthrow Mussolini
22 Jan 1944	Allied soldiers land at Anzio in Italy
4 Jun 1944	The Allies make it to Rome
6 Jun 1944	'D-Day' – Allied soldiers invade France
Feb 1945	The Americans land on the island of Iwo Jima, and win it after a very tough fight
Apr 1945	Hitler kills himself in his bunker in Berlin
8 May 1945	Victory in Europe is celebrated, otherwise known as VE Day
6 Aug 1945	'Little Boy' is dropped on Hiroshima
15 Aug 1945	After Japan surrenders to the Allies, 'VJ Day' (Victory in Japan) is celebrated. The war is over
Oct 1945	The United Nations is founded, to try to make sure all this never happens again . . .

QUIZ

1 Why did people call the First World War 'The Great War'?
- because it was great fun
- because it was so enormous

2 What did the Germans call the lightning-fast attacks they made on countries like Poland?

3 What major bad mood started when the world economy crashed in 1929?

4 What was the name of the club Hitler set up for young Nazis?

5 Where did hundreds of boats rescue British soldiers escaping from France?

6 What was Britain's high-tech-radio plane-detection system called?

7 What kept Londoners awake for fifty-eight nights in a row?

8 What new use did Londoners make of Underground stations in World War Two?

9 If Britain and its friends were called 'the Allies', what was Germany's side in the war called?

10 What sort of housewife could you keep in your pocket?

11 Which leader's name meant 'Man of Steel'?

12 What did deadly Finnish soldiers wear on their feet?

13 Which country did the 'Red Army' fight for?

14 What was the name given to Japanese suicide missions, meaning 'divine wind'?

15 Where was 'Churchill's Toy Shop'?

16 What was the Germans' top-secret code machine called?

17 What was the codename for the Allies' invasion of Europe?
- D-Day
- i-Day or
- X-Day?

ANSWERS 1) Because it was so enormous.
2) Blitzkrieg. 3) The Great Depression. 4) The Hitler Youth.
5) Dunkirk. 6) Radar. 7) The Blitz. 8) Air-raid shelters. 9) The Axis.
10) A sewing kit. 11) Stalin. 12) Skis. 13) Russia. 14) Kamikaze.
15) In the Natural History Museum. 16) Enigma. 17) D-Day.

Sir Tony Robinson's Weird World of Wonders is a multi-platform extravaganza (which doesn't mean it's a circus in a large railway station). You can get my World of Wonders game on line, there's a website, ebook, audio versions, extra stories and bits of weirdly wonderful design, marketing and publicity. In order to get all those things sorted out, I've surrounded myself with a grown-up version of the Curiosity Crew. They are Gaby Morgan and Fliss Stevens (Editorial), Dan Newman and Tracey Ridgewell (Design), Amy Lines (Marketing), Sally Oliphant (Publicity), James Luscombe (Digital), Tom Skipp (Ebooks) and Becky Lloyd (Audio). A big thanks to them all; they are committed, funny and extremely cool.

Tony has to say that otherwise they'd stop work and go home!

Also available in this series

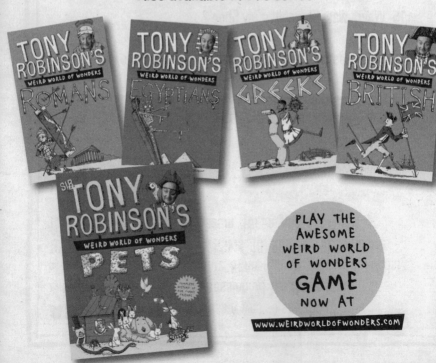

TONY ROBINSON'S WEIRD WORLD OF WONDERS ROMANS

TONY ROBINSON'S WEIRD WORLD OF WONDERS EGYPTIANS

TONY ROBINSON'S WEIRD WORLD OF WONDERS GREEKS

TONY ROBINSON'S WEIRD WORLD OF WONDERS BRITISH

SIR TONY ROBINSON'S WEIRD WORLD OF WONDERS PETS

PLAY THE AWESOME WEIRD WORLD OF WONDERS GAME NOW AT

WWW.WEIRDWORLDOFWONDERS.COM